# THE COMPLETE

## Air Fryer

# COOKBOOK
# UK 🇬🇧 2023

800 Days Healthy, Fresh and Foolproof Air Fryer Recipes for the Whole Family incl. Tasty Desserts Special

**800 DAYS RECIPES**

James Miles

**Warning-Disclaimer**

The purpose of this book is to educate and entertain. The author or publisher does not guarantee that anyone following the techniques, suggestions, tips, ideas, or strategies will become successful. The author and publisher shall have neither liability or responsibility to anyone with respect to any loss or damage caused, or alleged to be caused, directly or indirectly by the information contained in this book.

# Table of Content

## Chapter 5 Beef, Pork, and Lamb     30

## Chapter 6 Fish and Seafood     40

## Chapter 7 Vegetables and Sides     48

## Chapter 8 Snacks and Appetizers 55

## Chapter 9 Staples, Sauces, Dips, and Dressings 61

## Chapter 10 Holiday Specials 64

# INTRODUCTION

Cooking could get twice more fun and stress-free with that one perfect kitchen appliance! But how? We all know life is not all bed of roses, however, your kitchen experience could be. Cooking is an excellent activity and is very enjoyable when you don't have to wipe out beads of sweat from your forehead every second, and struggle between different appliances all at once.

Certain unique kitchen appliances can make your cooking experience seamless and organize your cooking process. And whether or not you're just setting up your kitchen space or you've established your area, you definitely will find the need for these cooking gems that automatically spur on your cooking creativity and makes a cooking genius out of you.

The air fryer is one of those brilliant kitchen inventions that bring all your cooking into one place and guarantee safe and healthy cooking. The gospel of this appliance has spread worldwide, with believing homeowners singing its praises and its benefits flying across all social media. It is an easy favourite among kitchen enthusiasts because its various features save energy and time and reduce calories.

Thus, what makes using the air fryer better than conventional cooking is the convenience involved and its health benefit, making it almost difficult for it to be a hated piece of appliance. The air fryer uses only little oil to bake, fry and grill, combining the features of about three devices in one compact body with more than 2x effectiveness. Plus, it lets you cook whatever you want at the time and temperature you want, perfectly and healthily.

You could never go wrong with an air fryer, and you must have your first doubts, just like I did; it is almost impossible for you not to. My air fryer sat in the corner of my kitchen for months without being used because I thought it was one of those junk you buy because of the hype and isn't that great. Well, you guessed it, after a few times of use, it was evident that this appliance isn't too good to be true, but too good and too true.

So, instead of having a deep fryer, an oven and a grilling machine filling up your kitchen space, you could get an air fryer that performs the work of these three perfectly. However, these other appliances have their perks and are most suitable for bigger cooking projects; the air fryer is your kitchen ally for cooking family-sized meals and mini-sized meals, depending on the appliance's capacity.

Want to know more about the air fryer? This book fully exposes all you need to know about the air fryer, the different meals you can make with it and how to unlock your cooking genius by trying out other meals with the air fryer. This book is a cook cheat book for every homemaker, armed with loads of mouth-watering recipes, easily accessible ingredients, and a step-by-step guide on how to cook these meals. You do not have to worry about whether you have years of cooking experience or are just trying out cooking. With these recipes and the air fryer, you're sure to become a genius in no time. Can't wait? Let's dive into it immediately.

# Chapter 1 Air Fryer Basic Guide

# Chapter 1 Air Fryer Basic Guide

The Air Fryer is a moderate-sized kitchen appliance similar to an oven and works as a deep fryer, as it bakes, roasts and fries everything from cookies and cakes to chicken and crispy chips. What makes the air fryer more convenient is its cooking methods; unlike a regular oven or deep fryer, it uses minimal to no oil and can be powered to cook at a particular time and the most suitable temperature. This kitchen appliance cooks by evenly regulating heat from a heat source on top of the air fryer, resulting in a healthy and perfectly cooked meal.

## How Does an Air Fryer Work?

Knowing your air fryer and its functionalities is vital to starting your journey as a kitchen creative. So, it is necessary to want to know how the air fryer works. An air fryer uses heat to cook with little or no oil, making the meal crispy and brown but gentle inside. Additionally, the appliance saves energy and time and makes your cooking less messy.

Some parts of the air fryer that generally contributes to its cooking functions are perforated baskets, holed ceramic plates, a drawer, a timer, a temperature dial and wire racks. In addition, some models of the air fryer come with preset recipes where you can cook certain everyday meals with just a single click of a button.

Here are the things you need to do before getting your air fryer to start cooking meals:

1. Unbox the appliance and place it on a rigid and heat-resistant surface.

2. Put the drawers and basket in their place.

3. Plug the air fryer into a power source.

4. You may clean out the air fryer's basket and drawer with soap and water and a dry cloth.

5. Then preheat the air fryer by setting the timer to 5 minutes and the temperature at 400 degrees Fahrenheit.

6. The timer stops when it is done cooking, and a beep goes off to indicate it is done.

7. You may draw out the basket by its handle and let it cool off before you start cooking!

## Five Features of the Air Fryer

This cooking companion possesses different features that sum up its awesomeness and make it a top topic in the cooking world, with its reputation for creating healthy meals quickly and seamlessly. Here are five unique features of the air fryer:

Less fat

An air fryer serves as a healthy substitution for deep fryers. It uses less oil in its cooking and significantly reduces the fat in food. Unlike deep-fried meals, which are high in fat as the food needs to be immersed in oil to be cooked properly, the air fryer does not need so much oil due to its unique cooking method. It uses an air-circulatory system that allows the food to cook just as perfect as it usually would. Health experts have commended this air fryer feature that both makes cooking easy and lets people eat healthily.

Faster meals

The convection heat element of the air fryer facilitates

quicker cooking. The heat is regulated quickly by a fan in its compact space and will reach cooking temperatures 2x faster than conventional ovens or deep fryers. Once you've set your timer and temperature, the air fryer starts cooking immediately, heats the air, and cooks meals in no time.

More meal choices

As I've stated earlier, the air fryer cooks everything from fluffy sweet cakes to french fries. You have plenty of options when it comes to cooking in an air fryer, and for specific models of the air fryer, you get to choose from a preset program and cook some meals by clicking a button. You may also heat meals and vegetables with this appliance. Furthermore, for larger air fryers, you can cook two different recipes simultaneously.

Less energy

Many people love the air fryer's ability to preserve energy. Although the amount of electricity the air fryer consumes depends on certain factors such as the type, temperature and timing it is used in, it has proven cheaper and less energy-consuming than regular ovens and electric cookers. This is because the air fryer requires only a few kilowatts to reach its maximum heat level and cook the meal perfectly, thus, saving energy and cost.

Enough capacity

An average-sized air fryer can cook a single meal at once. However, there are different sizes of air fryers depending on how much you cook. Small-sized, middle-sized, and family-sized air fryers are available, which cook with the same functions and efficiency.

## Different Types of Air Fryers

There are various types and numerous air fryer products in the market, so you may find it challenging to choose an ideal one. This article guides you on some of the different air fryer types and features that will make your decision-making easier. So, here we go:

1. Basket Air Fryer

The basket air fryer is one of the most common types of air fryer and also one of the first types. It comes in different shapes like round, cylindrical and round. However the shape or size, they all come with a removable basket that holds the food while the air fryer cooks. It also allows any excess oil in the food to drop into the drawer, making it entirely calorie-free. In addition, the basket has a handle to draw out and toss the food between cooking. A good example of this is the Tower T17021 family size Air Fryer that has 4 litre capacity with a dual basket and cooks a variety of meals quickly with 99% less fat.

2. Paddle Air Fryer

The stir-frying feature of the paddle air fryer makes it different from the basket air fryer. These air fryer styles come with a rotating paddle at the centre of the basket, which rotates while the food is cooking to ensure the even distribution of air and perfect cooking. So, you do not have to pull out the basket to check the progress of your meal every time, since the cookware makes sure your food is cooked well. All you need to do is set the time and temperature correctly and wait for your meal to cook. Additionally, this air fryer offers more meal options, as you can cook curries and saucy recipes. The Tefal ActiFry Genius XL 2-in-1 air fryer is an excellent paddle air fryer which is versatile and unique with functions that remind you when to add in ingredients while cooking. It has an additional container for double cooking and a preset program for specific meals.

3. Oven Air Fryer

An oven air fryer is a pretty versatile air fryer style. It comes in various shapes and sizes and looks like an oven with a rectangular shape. Although the functions and features of this air fryer are similar to the others, it extends its use further by being able to bake, broil, bake and dehydrate meals. Also, you do not have to draw out the basket to monitor it as in basket air fryers, as it has a glass door that allows you to see the activity inside the air fryer. Lastly, having quite a big rectangular rack, it accommodates different meals to be cooked simultaneously. So you can have an air fryer with a large capacity and more comprehensive meal options.

The Breville Halo Rotisserie air fryer oven is an excellent air fryer that perfectly cooks small chicken and has a chip basket for fries. It has a large capacity and is multifunctional.

4. Halogen Air Fryer

This air fryer works slightly differently from the others because its heat source is a halogen light that circulates the food. Its design doesn't allow it to shake the food, so you must do that yourself. However, halogen air fryers usually come with a large capacity to accommodate meals as big as a whole turkey. The Tower T14001 Health Halogen Low Fat Air Fryer is a good model in this category. It has a Removable Glass Bowl and is multifunctional having a large capacity. It also has a recipe book you will absolutely appreciate when you just begin making meals.

5. Pressure Cooker Air Fryer

This cookware is a combination of an air fryer and a pressure cooker. So if you need a pressure cooker that cooks crispy fries, bakes, roasts, and a few regular meals, then this air fryer is your 100% fit. Also, specific models of this air fryer can slow cook depending on how you want your meal prepared. The Ninja FD401 Foodi air fryer fulfills this category of air fryers; it has a large capacity that can cook a whole family meal. With 12 presets and two recipe books, you'll be ready to cook immediately you get your air fryer working.

## Air Fryer Cooking Tips

As we've discussed the efficacy and benefits of using the air fryer, you're almost ready to start making healthy and fantastic recipes with your air fryer. So, here are a few cooking tips which I've collated to help you start making meals and guide your everyday use:

◆ Always keep the air fryer on a heat-resistant surface in your kitchen and ensure that you place nothing on it.
◆ Add little water to the drawer of the fryer when making fatty meals, such as sausages and bacon, to prevent the grease from overheating and smoking.
◆ Toss and shake the food between cooking to allow it to brown perfectly.
◆ You may draw out the basket while you're cooking to check its progress from time to time; this doesn't distort the cooking process.
◆ Use a toothpick to hold down light food, such as bread slices on sandwiches, which may be blown around by the fan.
◆ To produce a more crispy and brownish result, you can add a bit of oil to the drawer.
◆ The drawer collects excess oil from the food, so do not turn the basket over after cooking while it's still attached to the drawer, as oil may spill.
◆ Use baking tins or oven dishes when baking cakes or light meals.
◆ Do not overcrowd the air fryer basket; putting too many meals in the basket at once will result in poorly cooked meals, as the air will not circulate properly.
◆ Small meals are easy to shake while cooking, so you may do this every few minutes while the air fryer is working to enhance even cooking.
◆ You can use the air fryer to reheat leftover meals.
◆ Different recipes require different timing and temperature. Some air fryer models have a user manual with appropriate timing and temperature for certain meals, so, you can refer to it if you are confused about how to do that.

## Care and Cleaning

When your meal is done, there's not much the air fryer does anymore; thus, it's time to put your air fryer to rest until you're ready to make your next meal. The first step is cleaning the appliance. It is vital to clean your air fryer just as you clean other kitchen appliances after use. It makes maintenance easy and contributes to the cookware's durability. So, here are some tips for cleaning the air fryer:

- ♦ Unplug the air fryer from the power source and wait for it to cool off for a bit.
- ♦ Then, pull out the basket and drawer and wash them with liquid soap, warm water, and a non-abrasive sponge.
- ♦ Wipe them with a clean towel after washing, or lay them aside to dry.
- ♦ Clean the inside of the air fryer with a damp soapy cloth and then dry it with a dry towel.
- ♦ Clean the exterior of the air fryer with a soft cloth and gently.
- ♦ Replace the basket and drawer to their position when they are dehydrated.
- ♦ Lastly, keep the appliance in a dry place.

## Air Fryer Questions & Answers

1.What cannot be cooked in the air fry?

As much as it's easy to say the air fryer can cook anything, some foods are not just suitable to be cooked in the air fryer. Some of these meals include battered meals because it is a wet food and will drip onto the drawer through the basket when cooked in the air fryer. Another is a large chicken, as the air will not circulate throughout the chicken, resulting in uneven cooking. Lastly, leafy greens may not just be a good idea to cook in an air fryer because the air circulation will make the leaves be blown all over and will not make any substantial effort to cook it.

2.How do I prevent food from sticking to the air fryer?

For food that sticks, like fish or breaded chicken, spray a light amount of vegetable oil on the basket. This will make sticking less likely.

3.How much food can an air fryer hold?

The air fryer comes in different sizes; how much yours can hold depends mainly on the size of the air fryer you have or wish to buy. A standard air fryer for home use can measure up to 5 to 10 quarts in capacity, but they're are also family sizes, up to 21 quarts. Therefore, an air fryer's capacity varies with size.

4.Can you cook with oil in an air fryer?

An air fryer needs minimal oil to cook and, sometimes, none. However, add little oil to the drawer for more crisp meals. You may also spray lightly on the food halfway through cooking. But, do not lose the drawer with oil as this could be hazardous.

# Chapter 2 Breakfasts

# Chapter 2 Breakfasts

## Ham and Cheese Crescents

**Prep time: 5 minutes | Cook time: 7 minutes | Makes 8 rolls**

Oil, for spraying
1 (230 g) can ready-to-bake croissants
4 slices wafer-thin ham

8 cheese slices
2 tablespoons unsalted butter, melted

Line the air fryer basket with parchment and spray lightly with oil. Separate the dough into 8 pieces.
Tear the ham slices in half and place 1 piece on each piece of dough. Top each with 1 slice of cheese.
Roll up each piece of dough, starting on the wider side.
Place the rolls in the prepared basket. Brush with the melted butter.
Air fry at 160°C for 6 to 7 minutes, or until puffed and golden brown and the cheese is melted.

## Bacon Eggs on the Go

**Prep time: 5 minutes | Cook time: 15 minutes | Serves 1**

2 eggs
110 g bacon, cooked

Salt and ground black pepper, to taste

Preheat the air fryer to 204°C. Put liners in a regular cupcake tin.
Crack an egg into each of the cups and add the bacon. Season with some pepper and salt.
Bake in the preheated air fryer for 15 minutes, or until the eggs are set. Serve warm.

## Hole in One

**Prep time: 5 minutes | Cook time: 6 to 7 minutes | Serves 1**

1 slice bread
1 teaspoon soft butter
1 egg
Salt and pepper, to taste

1 tablespoon shredded Cheddar cheese
2 teaspoons diced ham

Place a baking dish inside air fryer basket and preheat the air fryer to 166°C.
Using a 2½-inch-diameter biscuit cutter, cut a hole in center of bread slice.
Spread softened butter on both sides of bread.
Lay bread slice in baking dish and crack egg into the hole. Sprinkle egg with salt and pepper to taste.
Cook for 5 minutes.
Turn toast over and top it with shredded cheese and diced ham.
Cook for 1 to 2 more minutes or until yolk is done to your liking.

## Banana-Nut Muffins

**Prep time: 5 minutes | Cook time: 15 minutes | Makes 10 muffins**

Oil, for spraying
2 very ripe bananas
120 ml packed light brown sugar
80 ml rapeseed oil or vegetable oil

1 large egg
1 teaspoon vanilla extract
180 ml plain flour
1 teaspoon baking powder
1 teaspoon ground cinnamon
120 ml chopped walnuts

Preheat the air fryer to 160°C. Spray 10 silicone muffin cups lightly with oil.
In a medium bowl, mash the bananas. Add the brown sugar, rapeseed oil, egg, and vanilla and stir to combine.
Fold in the flour, baking powder, and cinnamon until just combined. Add the walnuts and fold a few times to distribute throughout the batter.
Divide the batter equally among the prepared muffin cups and place them in the basket. You may need to work in batches, depending on the size of your air fryer.
Cook for 15 minutes, or until golden brown and a toothpick inserted into the center of a muffin comes out clean. The air fryer tends to brown muffins more than the oven, so don't be alarmed if they are darker than you're used to. They will still taste great.
Let cool on a wire rack before serving.

## Spinach and Swiss Frittata with Mushrooms

**Prep time: 10 minutes | Cook time: 20 minutes | Serves 4**

Olive oil cooking spray
8 large eggs
½ teaspoon salt
½ teaspoon black pepper
1 garlic clove, minced
475 ml fresh baby spinach

110 g baby mushrooms, sliced
1 shallot, diced
120 ml shredded Swiss cheese, divided
Hot sauce, for serving (optional)

Preheat the air fryer to 182°C. Lightly coat the inside of a 6-inch round cake pan with olive oil cooking spray.
In a large bowl, beat the eggs, salt, pepper, and garlic for 1 to 2 minutes, or until well combined.
Fold in the spinach, mushrooms, shallot, and 60 ml the Swiss cheese.
Pour the egg mixture into the prepared cake pan, and sprinkle the remaining 60 ml Swiss over the top.
Place into the air fryer and bake for 18 to 20 minutes, or until the eggs are set in the center.
Remove from the air fryer and allow to cool for 5 minutes. Drizzle with hot sauce (if using) before serving.

## Tomato and Mozzarella Bruschetta

**Prep time: 5 minutes | Cook time: 4 minutes | Serves 1**

6 small loaf slices
120 ml tomatoes, finely chopped
85 g Mozzarella cheese, grated
1 tablespoon fresh basil, chopped
1 tablespoon olive oil

Preheat the air fryer to 176ºC.
Put the loaf slices inside the air fryer and air fry for about 3 minutes.
Add the tomato, Mozzarella, basil, and olive oil on top.
Air fry for an additional minute before serving.

## Oat Bran Muffins

**Prep time: 10 minutes | Cook time: 10 to 12 minutes per batch | Makes 8 muffins**

160 ml oat bran
120 ml flour
60 ml brown sugar
1 teaspoon baking powder
½ teaspoon baking soda
⅛ teaspoon salt
120 ml buttermilk
1 egg
2 tablespoons rapeseed oil
120 ml chopped dates, raisins, or dried cranberries
24 paper muffin cups
Cooking spray

Preheat the air fryer to 166ºC.
In a large bowl, combine the oat bran, flour, brown sugar, baking powder, baking soda, and salt.
In a small bowl, beat together the buttermilk, egg, and oil.
Pour buttermilk mixture into bowl with dry ingredients and stir just until moistened. Do not beat.
Gently stir in dried fruit.
Use triple baking cups to help muffins hold shape during baking. Spray them with cooking spray, place 4 sets of cups in air fryer basket at a time, and fill each one ¾ full of batter.
Cook for 10 to 12 minutes, until top springs back when lightly touched and toothpick inserted in center comes out clean.
Repeat for remaining muffins.

## Fried Chicken Wings with Waffles

**Prep time: 10 minutes | Cook time: 30 minutes | Serves 4**

8 whole chicken wings
1 teaspoon garlic powder
Chicken seasoning, for preparing the chicken
Freshly ground black pepper, to taste
120 ml plain flour
Cooking oil spray
8 frozen waffles
Pure maple syrup, for serving (optional)

1.In a medium bowl, combine the chicken and garlic powder and season with chicken seasoning and pepper. Toss to coat.
Transfer the chicken to a resealable plastic bag and add the flour. Seal the bag and shake it to coat the chicken thoroughly.
Insert the crisper plate into the basket and the basket into the unit. Preheat the unit by selecting AIR FRY, setting the temperature to 204ºC, and setting the time to 3 minutes. Select START/STOP to begin.
Once the unit is preheated, spray the crisper plate with cooking oil. Using tongs, transfer the chicken from the bag to the basket. It is okay to stack the chicken wings on top of each other. Spray them with cooking oil.
Select AIR FRY, set the temperature to 204ºC, and set the time to 20 minutes. Select START/STOP to begin.
After 5 minutes, remove the basket and shake the wings. Reinsert the basket to resume cooking. Remove and shake the basket every 5 minutes until the chicken is fully cooked.
When the cooking is complete, remove the cooked chicken from the basket; cover to keep warm.
Rinse the basket and crisper plate with warm water. Insert them back into the unit.
Select AIR FRY, set the temperature to 182ºC, and set the time to 3 minutes. Select START/STOP to begin.
Once the unit is preheated, spray the crisper plate with cooking spray. Working in batches, place the frozen waffles into the basket. Do not stack them. Spray the waffles with cooking oil.
Select AIR FRY, set the temperature to 182ºC, and set the time to 6 minutes. Select START/STOP to begin.
When the cooking is complete, repeat steps 10 and 11 with the remaining waffles.
Serve the waffles with the chicken and a touch of maple syrup, if desired.

## Apple Cider Doughnut Holes

**Prep time: 10 minutes | Cook time: 6 minutes | Makes 10 mini doughnuts**

Doughnut Holes:
350 ml plain flour
2 tablespoons granulated sugar
2 teaspoons baking powder
1 teaspoon baking soda
½ teaspoon coarse or flaky salt
Pinch of freshly grated nutmeg
60 ml plus 2 tablespoons buttermilk, chilled
2 tablespoons apple cider or
apple juice, chilled
1 large egg, lightly beaten
Vegetable oil, for brushing
Glaze:
120 ml icing sugar
2 tablespoons unsweetened applesauce
¼ teaspoon vanilla extract
Pinch of coarse or flaky salt

Make the doughnut holes: In a bowl, whisk together the flour, granulated sugar, baking powder, baking soda, salt, and nutmeg until smooth. Add the buttermilk, cider, and egg and stir with a small rubber spatula or spoon until the dough just comes together.
Using a 28 g ice cream scoop or 2 tablespoons, scoop and drop 10 balls of dough into the air fryer basket, spaced evenly apart, and brush the tops lightly with oil.
Air fry at 176ºC until the doughnut holes are golden brown and fluffy, about 6 minutes. Transfer the doughnut holes to a wire rack to cool completely.
Make the glaze: In a small bowl, stir together the powdered sugar, applesauce, vanilla, and salt until smooth.
Dip the tops of the doughnuts holes in the glaze, then let stand until the glaze sets before serving.
If you're impatient and want warm doughnuts, have the glaze ready to go while the doughnuts cook, then use the glaze as a dipping sauce for the warm doughnuts, fresh out of the air fryer.

# Three-Berry Dutch Pancake

**Prep time: 10 minutes | Cook time: 12 to 16 minutes | Serves 4**

2 egg whites
1 egg
120 ml wholemeal plain flour plus 1 tablespoon corn flour
120 ml semi-skimmed milk
1 teaspoon pure vanilla extract

1 tablespoon unsalted butter, melted
235 ml sliced fresh strawberries
120 ml fresh blueberries
120 ml fresh raspberries

In a medium bowl, use an eggbeater or hand mixer to quickly mix the egg whites, egg, flour, milk, and vanilla until well combined.
Use a pastry brush to grease the bottom of a baking pan with the melted butter. Immediately pour in the batter and put the basket back in the fryer.
Bake at 166°C for 12 to 16 minutes, or until the pancake is puffed and golden brown.
Remove the pan from the air fryer; the pancake will fall. Top with the strawberries, blueberries, and raspberries.
Serve immediately.

# Drop Biscuits

**Prep time: 10 minutes | Cook time: 9 to 10 minutes | Serves 5**

1 L plain flour
1 tablespoon baking powder
1 tablespoon sugar (optional)
1 teaspoon salt
6 tablespoons butter, plus more

for brushing on the biscuits (optional)
180 ml buttermilk
1 to 2 tablespoons oil

In a large bowl, whisk the flour, baking powder, sugar (if using), and salt until blended.
Add the butter. Using a pastry cutter or 2 forks, work the dough until pea-size balls of the butter-flour mixture appear. Stir in the buttermilk until the mixture is sticky.
Preheat the air fryer to 166°C. Line the air fryer basket with parchment paper and spritz it with oil.
Drop the dough by the tablespoonful onto the prepared basket, leaving 1 inch between each, to form 10 biscuits.
Bake for 5 minutes. Flip the biscuits and cook for 4 minutes more for a light brown top, or 5 minutes more for a darker biscuit. Brush the tops with melted butter, if desired.

# Spinach and Bacon Roll-ups

**Prep time: 5 minutes | Cook time: 8 to 9 minutes | Serves 4**

4 flour tortillas (6- or 7-inch size)
4 slices Swiss cheese
235 ml baby spinach leaves

4 slices turkey bacon
Special Equipment:
4 toothpicks, soak in water for at least 30 minutes

Preheat the air fryer to 200°C.
On a clean work surface, top each tortilla with one slice of cheese and 60 ml spinach, then tightly roll them up.
Wrap each tortilla with a strip of turkey bacon and secure with a toothpick.
Arrange the roll-ups in the air fryer basket, leaving space between each roll-up.
Air fry for 4 minutes.
Flip the roll-ups with tongs and rearrange them for more even cooking. Air fry for another 4 to 5 minutes until the bacon is crisp.
Rest for 5 minutes and remove the toothpicks before serving.

# Blueberry Cobbler

**Prep time: 5 minutes | Cook time: 15 minutes | Serves 4**

80 ml wholemeal pastry flour
¾ teaspoon baking powder
Dash sea salt
120 ml semi-skimmed milk
2 tablespoons pure maple syrup

½ teaspoon vanilla extract
Cooking oil spray
120 ml fresh blueberries
60 ml granola

In a medium bowl, whisk the flour, baking powder, and salt. Add the milk, maple syrup, and vanilla and gently whisk, just until thoroughly combined.
Preheat the unit by selecting BAKE, setting the temperature to 176°C, and setting the time to 3 minutes. Select START/STOP to begin.
Spray a 6-by-2-inch round baking pan with cooking oil and pour the batter into the pan. Top evenly with the blueberries and granola. Once the unit is preheated, place the pan into the basket.
Select BAKE, set the temperature to 176°C, and set the time to 15 minutes. Select START/STOP to begin.
When the cooking is complete, the cobbler should be nicely browned and a knife inserted into the middle should come out clean.
Enjoy plain or topped with a little vanilla yoghurt.

# Quesadillas

**Prep time: 10 minutes | Cook time: 15 minutes | Serves 4**

4 eggs
2 tablespoons skimmed milk
Salt and pepper, to taste
Oil for misting or cooking spray
4 flour tortillas

4 tablespoons salsa
60 g Cheddar cheese, grated
½ small avocado, peeled and thinly sliced

Preheat the air fryer to 132°C.
Beat together eggs, milk, salt, and pepper.
Spray a baking pan lightly with cooking spray and add egg mixture.
Bake for 8 to 9 minutes, stirring every 1 to 2 minutes, until eggs are scrambled to your liking. Remove and set aside.
Spray one side of each tortilla with oil or cooking spray. Flip over.
Divide eggs, salsa, cheese, and avocado among the tortillas, covering only half of each tortilla.
Fold each tortilla in half and press down lightly.
Place 2 tortillas in air fryer basket and air fry at 200°C for 3 minutes or until cheese melts and outside feels slightly crispy. Repeat with remaining two tortillas.
Cut each cooked tortilla into halves or thirds.

## Bacon Cheese Egg with Avocado

**Prep time: 15 minutes | Cook time: 20 minutes | Serves 4**

6 large eggs
60 ml double cream
350 ml chopped cauliflower
235 ml shredded medium
Cheddar cheese
1 medium avocado, peeled and
pitted

8 tablespoons full-fat sour
cream
2 spring onions, sliced on the
bias
12 slices bacon, cooked and
crumbled

In a medium bowl, whisk eggs and cream together. Pour into a round baking dish.
Add cauliflower and mix, then top with Cheddar. Place dish into the air fryer basket.
Adjust the temperature to 160ºC and set the timer for 20 minutes.
When completely cooked, eggs will be firm and cheese will be browned. Slice into four pieces.
Slice avocado and divide evenly among pieces. Top each piece with 2 tablespoons sour cream, sliced spring onions, and crumbled bacon.

## Red Pepper and Feta Frittata

**Prep time: 10 minutes | Cook time: 20 minutes | Serves 4**

Olive oil cooking spray
8 large eggs
1 medium red pepper, diced
½ teaspoon salt

½ teaspoon black pepper
1 garlic clove, minced
120 ml feta, divided

Preheat the air fryer to 182ºC. Lightly coat the inside of a 6-inch round cake pan with olive oil cooking spray.
In a large bowl, beat the eggs for 1 to 2 minutes, or until well combined.
Add the red pepper, salt, black pepper, and garlic to the eggs, and mix together until the red pepper is distributed throughout.
Fold in 60 ml the feta cheese.
Pour the egg mixture into the prepared cake pan, and sprinkle the remaining 60 ml feta over the top.
Place into the air fryer and bake for 18 to 20 minutes, or until the eggs are set in the center.
Remove from the air fryer and allow to cool for 5 minutes before serving.

## Maple Granola

**Prep time: 5 minutes | Cook time: 40 minutes | Makes 475 ml**

235 ml rolled oats
3 tablespoons pure maple syrup
1 tablespoon sugar
1 tablespoon neutral-flavored
oil, such as refined coconut or

sunflower
¼ teaspoon sea salt
¼ teaspoon ground cinnamon
¼ teaspoon vanilla extract

Insert the crisper plate into the basket and the basket into the unit.
Preheat the unit by selecting BAKE, setting the temperature to 120ºC, and setting the time to 3 minutes. Select START/STOP to begin.
In a medium bowl, stir together the oats, maple syrup, sugar, oil, salt, cinnamon, and vanilla until thoroughly combined. Transfer the granola to a 6-by-2-inch round baking pan.
Once the unit is preheated, place the pan into the basket.
Select BAKE, set the temperature to 120ºC and set the time to 40 minutes. Select START/STOP to begin.
After 10 minutes, stir the granola well. Resume cooking, stirring the granola every 10 minutes, for a total of 40 minutes, or until the granola is lightly browned and mostly dry.
When the cooking is complete, place the granola on a plate to cool. It will become crisp as it cools. Store the completely cooled granola in an airtight container in a cool, dry place for 1 to 2 weeks.

## Cheddar-Ham-Corn Muffins

**Prep time: 10 minutes | Cook time: 6 to 8 minutes per batch | Makes 8 muffins**

180 ml cornmeal/polenta
60 ml flour
1½ teaspoons baking powder
¼ teaspoon salt
1 egg, beaten
2 tablespoons rapeseed oil
120 ml milk

120 ml shredded sharp Cheddar
cheese
120 ml diced ham
8 foil muffin cups, liners
removed and sprayed with
cooking spray

Preheat the air fryer to 200ºC.
In a medium bowl, stir together the cornmeal, flour, baking powder, and salt.
Add egg, oil, and milk to dry ingredients and mix well.
Stir in shredded cheese and diced ham.
Divide batter among the muffin cups.
Place 4 filled muffin cups in air fryer basket and bake for 5 minutes. Reduce temperature to 166ºC and bake for 1 to 2 minutes or until toothpick inserted in center of muffin comes out clean.
Repeat steps 6 and 7 to cook remaining muffins.

## Not-So-English Muffins

**Prep time: 5 minutes | Cook time: 10 minutes | Serves 4**

2 strips turkey bacon, cut in half
crosswise
2 whole-grain English muffins,
split
235 ml fresh baby spinach, long
stems removed

¼ ripe pear, peeled and thinly
sliced
4 slices low-moisture
Mozzarella or other melting
cheese

Place bacon strips in air fryer basket and air fry at 200ºC for 2 minutes. Check and separate strips if necessary so they cook evenly. Cook for 3 to 4 more minutes, until crispy. Remove and drain on paper towels.
Place split muffin halves in air fryer basket and cook for 2 minutes, just until lightly browned.
Open air fryer and top each muffin with a quarter of the baby spinach, several pear slices, a strip of bacon, and a slice of cheese.
Air fry at 182ºC for 1 to 2 minutes, until cheese completely melts.

# Cheesy Bell Pepper Eggs

**Prep time: 10 minutes | Cook time: 15 minutes | Serves 4**

| | |
|---|---|
| 4 medium green peppers | chopped |
| 85 g cooked ham, chopped | 8 large eggs |
| ¼ medium onion, peeled and | 235 ml mild Cheddar cheese |

Cut the tops off each pepper. Remove the seeds and the white membranes with a small knife. Place ham and onion into each pepper.
Crack 2 eggs into each pepper. Top with 60 ml cheese per pepper. Place into the air fryer basket.
Adjust the temperature to 200°C and air fry for 15 minutes.
When fully cooked, peppers will be tender and eggs will be firm. Serve immediately.

# Baked Peach Oatmeal

**Prep time: 5 minutes | Cook time: 30 minutes | Serves 6**

| | |
|---|---|
| Olive oil cooking spray | 120 ml non-fat plain Greek |
| 475 ml certified gluten-free | yoghurt |
| rolled oats | 1 teaspoon vanilla extract |
| 475 ml unsweetened almond | ½ teaspoon ground cinnamon |
| milk | ¼ teaspoon salt |
| 60 ml honey, plus more for | 350 ml diced peaches, divided, |
| drizzling (optional) | plus more for serving (optional) |

Preheat the air fryer to 192°C. Lightly coat the inside of a 6-inch cake pan with olive oil cooking spray.
In a large bowl, mix together the oats, almond milk, honey, yoghurt, vanilla, cinnamon, and salt until well combined.
Fold in 180 ml peaches and then pour the mixture into the prepared cake pan.
Sprinkle the remaining peaches across the top of the oatmeal mixture. Bake in the air fryer for 30 minutes.
Allow to set and cool for 5 minutes before serving with additional fresh fruit and honey for drizzling, if desired.

# Cheddar Eggs

**Prep time: 5 minutes | Cook time: 15 minutes | Serves 2**

| | |
|---|---|
| 4 large eggs | 120 ml shredded sharp Cheddar |
| 2 tablespoons unsalted butter, | cheese |
| melted | |

Crack eggs into a round baking dish and whisk. Place dish into the air fryer basket.
Adjust the temperature to 204°C and set the timer for 10 minutes.
After 5 minutes, stir the eggs and add the butter and cheese. Let cook 3 more minutes and stir again.
Allow eggs to finish cooking an additional 2 minutes or remove if they are to your desired liking.
Use a fork to fluff. Serve warm.

# Spinach Omelet

**Prep time: 5 minutes | Cook time: 12 minutes | Serves 2**

| | |
|---|---|
| 4 large eggs | 2 tablespoons salted butter, |
| 350 ml chopped fresh spinach | melted |
| leaves | 120 ml shredded mild Cheddar |
| 2 tablespoons peeled and | cheese |
| chopped brown onion | ¼ teaspoon salt |

In an ungreased round nonstick baking dish, whisk eggs. Stir in spinach, onion, butter, Cheddar, and salt.
Place dish into air fryer basket. Adjust the temperature to 160°C and bake for 12 minutes. Omelet will be done when browned on the top and firm in the middle.
Slice in half and serve warm on two medium plates.

# Butternut Squash and Ricotta Frittata

**Prep time: 10 minutes | Cook time: 33 minutes | Serves 2 to 3**

| | |
|---|---|
| 235 ml cubed (½-inch) butternut | 4 fresh sage leaves, thinly sliced |
| squash (160 g) | 6 large eggs, lightly beaten |
| 2 tablespoons olive oil | 120 ml ricotta cheese |
| Coarse or flaky salt and freshly | Cayenne pepper |
| ground black pepper, to taste | |

In a bowl, toss the squash with the olive oil and season with salt and black pepper until evenly coated. Sprinkle the sage on the bottom of a cake pan and place the squash on top.
Place the pan in the air fryer and bake at 204°C for 10 minutes. Stir to incorporate the sage, then cook until the squash is tender and lightly caramelized at the edges, about 3 minutes more.
Pour the eggs over the squash, dollop the ricotta all over, and sprinkle with cayenne. Bake at 150°C until the eggs are set and the frittata is golden brown on top, about 20 minutes. Remove the pan from the air fryer and cut the frittata into wedges to serve.

# Parmesan Ranch Risotto

**Prep time: 10 minutes | Cook time: 30 minutes | Serves 2**

| | |
|---|---|
| 1 tablespoon olive oil | 180 ml Arborio rice |
| 1 clove garlic, minced | 475 ml chicken stock, boiling |
| 1 tablespoon unsalted butter | 120 ml Parmesan cheese, grated |
| 1 onion, diced | |

Preheat the air fryer to 200°C.
Grease a round baking tin with olive oil and stir in the garlic, butter, and onion.
Transfer the tin to the air fryer and bake for 4 minutes. Add the rice and bake for 4 more minutes.
Turn the air fryer to 160°C and pour in the chicken stock. Cover and bake for 22 minutes.
Scatter with cheese and serve.

# Gluten-Free Granola Cereal

**Prep time: 7 minutes | Cook time: 30 minutes | Makes 820 ml**

Oil, for spraying
350 ml gluten-free rolled oats
120 ml chopped walnuts
120 ml chopped almonds
120 ml pumpkin seeds
60 ml maple syrup or honey

1 tablespoon toasted sesame oil or vegetable oil
1 teaspoon ground cinnamon
½ teaspoon salt
120 ml dried cranberries

Preheat the air fryer to 120°C. Line the air fryer basket with parchment and spray lightly with oil. (Do not skip the step of lining the basket; the parchment will keep the granola from falling through the holes.)

In a large bowl, mix together the oats, walnuts, almonds, pumpkin seeds, maple syrup, sesame oil, cinnamon, and salt.

Spread the mixture in an even layer in the prepared basket.

Cook for 30 minutes, stirring every 10 minutes.

Transfer the granola to a bowl, add the dried cranberries, and toss to combine.

Let cool to room temperature before storing in an airtight container.

# Cajun Breakfast Sausage

**Prep time: 10 minutes | Cook time: 15 to 20 minutes | Serves 8**

680 g 85% lean turkey mince
3 cloves garlic, finely chopped
¼ onion, grated
1 teaspoon Tabasco sauce

1 teaspoon Cajun seasoning
1 teaspoon dried thyme
½ teaspoon paprika
½ teaspoon cayenne

Preheat the air fryer to 188°C.

In a large bowl, combine the turkey, garlic, onion, Tabasco, Cajun seasoning, thyme, paprika, and cayenne. Mix with clean hands until thoroughly combined. Shape into 16 patties, about ½ inch thick. (Wet your hands slightly if you find the sausage too sticky to handle.)

Working in batches if necessary, arrange the patties in a single layer in the air fryer basket. Pausing halfway through the cooking time to flip the patties, air fry for 15 to 20 minutes until a thermometer inserted into the thickest portion registers 74°C.

# Berry Muffins

**Prep time: 15 minutes | Cook time: 12 to 17 minutes | Makes 8**

muffins
315 ml plus 1 tablespoon plain flour, divided
60 ml granulated sugar
2 tablespoons light brown sugar

2 teaspoons baking powder
2 eggs
160 ml whole milk
80 ml neutral oil
235 ml mixed fresh berries

In a medium bowl, stir together 315 ml of flour, the granulated sugar, brown sugar, and baking powder until mixed well.

In a small bowl, whisk the eggs, milk, and oil until combined. Stir the egg mixture into the dry ingredients just until combined.

In another small bowl, toss the mixed berries with the remaining 1 tablespoon of flour until coated. Gently stir the berries into the batter.

Double up 16 foil muffin cups to make 8 cups.

Insert the crisper plate into the basket and the basket into the unit. Preheat the unit by selecting BAKE, setting the temperature to 156°C, and setting the time to 3 minutes. Select START/STOP to begin.

Once the unit is preheated, place 1 L into the basket and fill each three-quarters full with the batter.

Select BAKE, set the temperature to 156°C, and set the time for 17 minutes. Select START/STOP to begin.

After about 12 minutes, check the muffins. If they spring back when lightly touched with your finger, they are done. If not, resume cooking.

When the cooking is done, transfer the muffins to a wire rack to cool.1Repeat steps 6, 7, and 8 with the remaining muffin cups and batter.1Let the muffins cool for 10 minutes before serving.

# Denver Omelette

**Prep time: 5 minutes | Cook time: 8 minutes | Serves 1**

2 large eggs
60 ml unsweetened, unflavoured almond milk
¼ teaspoon fine sea salt
⅛ teaspoon ground black pepper
60 ml diced ham (omit for vegetarian)
60 ml diced green and red

peppers
2 tablespoons diced spring onions, plus more for garnish
60 ml shredded Cheddar cheese (about 30 g) (omit for dairy-free)
Quartered cherry tomatoes, for serving (optional)

Preheat the air fryer to 176°C. Grease a cake pan and set aside.

In a small bowl, use a fork to whisk together the eggs, almond milk, salt, and pepper. Add the ham, peppers, and spring onions. Pour the mixture into the greased pan. Add the cheese on top (if using).

Place the pan in the basket of the air fryer. Bake for 8 minutes, or until the eggs are cooked to your liking.

Loosen the omelette from the sides of the pan with a spatula and place it on a serving plate. Garnish with spring onions and serve with cherry tomatoes, if desired.

Best served fresh.

# Bacon, Cheese, and Avocado Melt

**Prep time: 5 minutes | Cook time: 3 to 5 minutes | Serves 2**

1 avocado
4 slices cooked bacon, chopped
2 tablespoons salsa

1 tablespoon double cream
60 ml shredded Cheddar cheese

Preheat the air fryer to 204°C.

Slice the avocado in half lengthwise and remove the stone. To ensure the avocado halves do not roll in the basket, slice a thin piece of skin off the base.

In a small bowl, combine the bacon, salsa, and cream. Divide the mixture between the avocado halves and top with the cheese.

Place the avocado halves in the air fryer basket and air fry for 3 to 5 minutes until the cheese has melted and begins to brown. Serve warm.

# Chapter 3 Vegetarian Mains

# Chapter 3 Vegetarian Mains

## Baked Courgette

**Prep time: 10 minutes | Cook time: 8 minutes | Serves 4**

2 tablespoons salted butter
60 ml diced white onion
½ teaspoon minced garlic
120 ml double cream

60 g full fat soft white cheese
235 ml shredded extra mature
Cheddar cheese
2 medium courgette, spiralized

In a large saucepan over medium heat, melt butter.
Add onion and sauté until it begins to soften, 1 to 3 minutes.
Add garlic and sauté for 30 seconds, then pour in cream and add soft white cheese.
Remove the pan from heat and stir in Cheddar.
Add the courgette and toss in the sauce, then put into a round baking dish.
Cover the dish with foil and place into the air fryer basket.
Adjust the temperature to 188ºC and set the timer for 8 minutes.
After 6 minutes remove the foil and let the top brown for remaining cooking time.
Stir and serve.

## Garlicky Sesame Carrots

**Prep time: 5 minutes | Cook time: 16 minutes | Serves 4 to 6**

450 g baby carrots
1 tablespoon sesame oil
½ teaspoon dried dill
Pinch salt

Freshly ground black pepper, to
taste
6 cloves garlic, peeled
3 tablespoons sesame seeds

Preheat the air fryer to 192ºC.
In a medium bowl, drizzle the baby carrots with the sesame oil.
Sprinkle with the dill, salt, and pepper and toss to coat well.
Place the baby carrots in the air fryer basket and roast for 8 minutes.
Remove the basket and stir in the garlic.
Return the basket to the air fryer and roast for another 8 minutes, or until the carrots are lightly browned.
Serve sprinkled with the sesame seeds.

## Gold Ravioli

**Prep time: 10 minutes | Cook time: 6 minutes | Serves 4**

120 ml panko breadcrumbs
2 teaspoons Engevita yeast
flakes
1 teaspoon dried basil
1 teaspoon dried oregano
1 teaspoon garlic powder

Salt and ground black pepper, to
taste
60 ml aquafaba or egg
alternative
227 g ravioli
Cooking spray

Cover the air fryer basket with aluminium foil and coat with a light brushing of oil.
Preheat the air fryer to 204ºC.
Combine the panko breadcrumbs, Engevita yeast flakes, basil, oregano, and garlic powder.
Sprinkle with salt and pepper to taste.
Put the aquafaba in a separate bowl.
Dip the ravioli in the aquafaba before coating it in the panko mixture.
Spritz with cooking spray and transfer to the air fryer.
Air fry for 6 minutes.
Shake the air fryer basket halfway.
Serve hot.

## Baked Turnip and Courgette

**Prep time: 5 minutes | Cook time: 15 to 20 minutes | Serves 4**

3 turnips, sliced
1 large courgette, sliced
1 large red onion, cut into rings

2 cloves garlic, crushed
1 tablespoon olive oil
Salt and black pepper, to taste

Preheat the air fryer to 166ºC.
Put the turnips, courgette, red onion, and garlic in a baking pan.
Drizzle the olive oil over the top and sprinkle with the salt and pepper.
Place the baking pan in the preheated air fryer and bake for 15 to 20 minutes, or until the vegetables are tender.
Remove from the basket and serve on a plate.

## White Cheddar and Mushroom Soufflés

**Prep time: 15 minutes | Cook time: 12 minutes | Serves 4**

3 large eggs, whites and yolks
separated
120 ml extra mature white
Cheddar cheese
85 g soft white cheese

¼ teaspoon cream of tartar
¼ teaspoon salt
¼ teaspoon ground black pepper
120 ml chestnut mushrooms,
sliced

In a large bowl, whip egg whites until stiff peaks form, about 2 minutes.
In a separate large bowl, beat Cheddar, egg yolks, soft white cheese, cream of tartar, salt, and pepper together until combined.
Fold egg whites into cheese mixture, being careful not to stir.
Fold in mushrooms, then pour mixture evenly into four ungreased ramekins.
Place ramekins into air fryer basket.
Adjust the temperature to 176ºC and bake for 12 minutes.
Eggs will be browned on the top and firm in the centre when done.
Serve warm.

## Roasted Vegetable Mélange with Herbs

**Prep time: 10 minutes | Cook time: 14 to 18 minutes | Serves 4**

1 (230 g) package sliced mushrooms
1 yellow butternut squash, sliced
1 red pepper, sliced

3 cloves garlic, sliced
1 tablespoon olive oil
½ teaspoon dried basil
½ teaspoon dried thyme
½ teaspoon dried tarragon

Preheat the air fryer to 176ºC.
Toss the mushrooms, squash, and pepper with the garlic and olive oil in a large bowl until well coated.
Mix in the basil, thyme, and tarragon and toss again.
Spread the vegetables evenly in the air fryer basket and roast for 14 to 18 minutes, or until the vegetables are fork-tender.
Cool for 5 minutes before serving.
Cheesy Cauliflower Pizza Crust
Prep time: 15 minutes | Cook time: 11 minutes | Serves 2
1 (340 g) steamer bag cauliflower
120 ml shredded extra mature Cheddar cheese
1 large egg
2 tablespoons blanched finely ground almond flour
1 teaspoon Italian blend seasoning

Cook cauliflower according to package instructions. Remove from bag and place into cheesecloth or paper towel to remove excess water.
Place cauliflower into a large bowl. Add cheese, egg, almond flour, and Italian seasoning to the bowl and mix well.
Cut a piece of parchment to fit your air fryer basket. Press cauliflower into 6-inch round circle. Place into the air fryer basket. Adjust the temperature to 182ºC and air fry for 11 minutes. After 7 minutes, flip the pizza crust. Add preferred toppings to pizza.
Place back into air fryer basket and cook an additional 4 minutes or until fully cooked and golden.
Serve immediately.

## Herbed Broccoli with Cheese

**Prep time: 5 minutes | Cook time: 18 minutes | Serves 4**

1 large-sized head broccoli, stemmed and cut into small florets
2½ tablespoons rapeseed oil
2 teaspoons dried basil

2 teaspoons dried rosemary
Salt and ground black pepper, to taste
80 ml grated yellow cheese

Bring a pot of lightly salted water to a boil.
Add the broccoli florets to the boiling water and let boil for about 3 minutes.
Drain the broccoli florets well and transfer to a large bowl.
Add the rapeseed oil, basil, rosemary, salt, and black pepper to the bowl and toss until the broccoli is fully coated.
Preheat the air fryer to 200ºC.
Place the broccoli in the air fryer basket and air fry for about 15 minutes, shaking the basket halfway through, or until the broccoli is crisp.
Serve the broccoli warm with grated cheese sprinkled on top.

## Cheesy Cabbage Wedges

**Prep time: 5 minutes | Cook time: 20 minutes | Serves 4**

4 tablespoons melted butter
1 head cabbage, cut into wedges
235 ml shredded Parmesan cheese

Salt and black pepper, to taste
120 ml shredded Mozzarella cheese

Preheat the air fryer to 192ºC.
Brush the melted butter over the cut sides of cabbage wedges and sprinkle both sides with the Parmesan cheese.
Season with salt and pepper to taste.
Place the cabbage wedges in the air fryer basket and air fry for 20 minutes, flipping the cabbage halfway through, or until the cabbage wedges are lightly browned.
Transfer the cabbage wedges to a plate and serve with the Mozzarella cheese sprinkled on top.

## Garlic White Courgette Rolls

**Prep time: 20 minutes | Cook time: 20 minutes | Serves 4**

2 medium courgette
2 tablespoons unsalted butter
¼ white onion, peeled and diced
½ teaspoon finely minced roasted garlic
60 ml double cream
2 tablespoons vegetable broth
⅛ teaspoon xanthan gum
120 ml full-fat ricotta cheese

¼ teaspoon salt
½ teaspoon garlic powder
¼ teaspoon dried oregano
475 ml spinach, chopped
120 ml sliced baby portobello mushrooms
180 ml shredded Mozzarella cheese, divided

Using a mandoline or sharp knife, slice courgette into long strips lengthwise.
Place strips between paper towels to absorb moisture. Set aside.
In a medium saucepan over medium heat, melt butter. Add onion and sauté until fragrant.
Add garlic and sauté 30 seconds. Pour in double cream, broth, and xanthan gum.
Turn off heat and whisk mixture until it begins to thicken, about 3 minutes.
In a medium bowl, add ricotta, salt, garlic powder, and oregano and mix well.
Fold in spinach, mushrooms, and 120 ml Mozzarella.
Pour half of the sauce into a round baking pan. To assemble the rolls, place two strips of courgette on a work surface. Spoon 2 tablespoons of ricotta mixture onto the slices and roll up.
Place seam side down on top of sauce. Repeat with remaining ingredients.
Pour remaining sauce over the rolls and sprinkle with remaining Mozzarella.
Cover with foil and place into the air fryer basket.
Adjust the temperature to 176ºC and bake for 20 minutes. In the last 5 minutes, remove the foil to brown the cheese.
Serve immediately.

## Stuffed Portobellos

**Prep time: 10 minutes | Cook time: 8 minutes | Serves 4**

85 g soft white cheese
½ medium courgette, trimmed and chopped
60 ml seeded and chopped red pepper
350 ml chopped fresh spinach

leaves
4 large portobello mushrooms, stems removed
2 tablespoons coconut oil, melted
½ teaspoon salt

In a medium bowl, mix soft white cheese, courgette, pepper, and spinach.
Drizzle mushrooms with coconut oil and sprinkle with salt.
Scoop ¼ courgette mixture into each mushroom. Place mushrooms into ungreased air fryer basket.
Adjust the temperature to 204°C and air fry for 8 minutes.
Portobellos will be tender, and tops will be browned when done.
Serve warm.

## Mushroom and Pepper Pizza Squares

**Prep time: 10 minutes | Cook time: 10 minutes | Serves 10**

1 pizza dough, cut into squares
235 ml chopped oyster mushrooms
1 shallot, chopped

¼ red pepper, chopped
2 tablespoons parsley
Salt and ground black pepper, to taste

Preheat the air fryer to 204°C.
In a bowl, combine the oyster mushrooms, shallot, pepper and parsley.
Sprinkle some salt and pepper as desired.
Spread this mixture on top of the pizza squares.
Bake in the air fryer for 10 minutes.
Serve warm.

## Roasted Vegetables with Rice

**Prep time: 5 minutes | Cook time: 12 minutes | Serves 4**

2 teaspoons melted butter
235 ml chopped mushrooms
235 ml cooked rice
235 ml peas
1 carrot, chopped

1 red onion, chopped
1 garlic clove, minced
Salt and black pepper, to taste
2 hard-boiled eggs, grated
1 tablespoon soy sauce

Preheat the air fryer to 192°C.
Coat a baking dish with melted butter.
Stir together the mushrooms, cooked rice, peas, carrot, onion, garlic, salt, and pepper in a large bowl until well mixed.
Pour the mixture into the prepared baking dish and transfer to the air fryer basket.
Roast in the preheated air fryer for 12 minutes until the vegetables are tender.
Divide the mixture among four plates.
Serve warm with a sprinkle of grated eggs and a drizzle of soy sauce.

## Caprese Aubergine Stacks

**Prep time: 5 minutes | Cook time: 12 minutes | Serves 4**

1 medium aubergine, cut into ¼-inch slices
2 large tomatoes, cut into ¼-inch slices

110 g fresh Mozzarella, cut into 14 g slices
2 tablespoons olive oil
60 ml fresh basil, sliced

In a baking dish, place four slices of aubergine on the bottom.
Place a slice of tomato on top of each aubergine round, then Mozzarella, then aubergine.
Repeat as necessary.
Drizzle with olive oil.
Cover dish with foil and place dish into the air fryer basket.
Adjust the temperature to 176°C and bake for 12 minutes.
When done, aubergine will be tender.
Garnish with fresh basil to serve.

## Italian Baked Egg and Veggies

**Prep time: 10 minutes | Cook time: 10 minutes | Serves 2**

2 tablespoons salted butter
1 small courgette, sliced lengthwise and quartered
½ medium green pepper, seeded and diced
235 ml fresh spinach, chopped

1 medium plum tomato, diced
2 large eggs
¼ teaspoon onion powder
¼ teaspoon garlic powder
½ teaspoon dried basil
¼ teaspoon dried oregano

Grease two ramekins with 1 tablespoon butter each.
In a large bowl, toss courgette, pepper, spinach, and tomato.
Divide the mixture in two and place half in each ramekin.
Crack an egg on top of each ramekin and sprinkle with onion powder, garlic powder, basil, and oregano.
Place into the air fryer basket.
Adjust the temperature to 166°C and bake for 10 minutes.
Serve immediately.

## Broccoli with Garlic Sauce

**Prep time: 19 minutes | Cook time: 15 minutes | Serves 4**

2 tablespoons olive oil
Rock salt and freshly ground black pepper, to taste
450 g broccoli florets
Dipping Sauce:
2 teaspoons dried rosemary,

crushed
3 garlic cloves, minced
⅓ teaspoon dried marjoram, crushed
60 ml sour cream
80 ml mayonnaise

Lightly grease your broccoli with a thin layer of olive oil.
Season with salt and ground black pepper.
Arrange the seasoned broccoli in the air fryer basket.
Bake at 202°C for 15 minutes, shaking once or twice.
In the meantime, prepare the dipping sauce by mixing all the sauce ingredients.
Serve warm broccoli with the dipping sauce and enjoy!

## Spinach-Artichoke Stuffed Mushrooms

**Prep time: 10 minutes | Cook time: 10 to 14 minutes | Serves 4**

2 tablespoons olive oil
4 large portobello mushrooms, stems removed and gills scraped out
½ teaspoon salt
¼ teaspoon freshly ground pepper
110 g goat cheese, crumbled

120 ml chopped marinated artichoke hearts
235 ml frozen spinach, thawed and squeezed dry
120 ml grated Parmesan cheese
2 tablespoons chopped fresh parsley

Preheat the air fryer to 204°C.
Rub the olive oil over the portobello mushrooms until thoroughly coated.
Sprinkle both sides with the salt and black pepper.
Place top-side down on a clean work surface.
In a small bowl, combine the goat cheese, artichoke hearts, and spinach.
Mash with the back of a fork until thoroughly combined.
Divide the cheese mixture among the mushrooms and sprinkle with the Parmesan cheese.
Air fry for 10 to 14 minutes until the mushrooms are tender and the cheese has begun to brown.
Top with the fresh parsley just before serving.

## Lush Summer Rolls

**Prep time: 15 minutes | Cook time: 15 minutes | Serves 4**

235 ml shiitake mushroom, sliced thinly
1 celery stalk, chopped
1 medium carrot, shredded
½ teaspoon finely chopped ginger

1 teaspoon sugar
1 tablespoon soy sauce
1 teaspoon Engevita yeast flakes
8 spring roll sheets
1 teaspoon corn starch
2 tablespoons water

In a bowl, combine the ginger, soy sauce, Engevita yeast flakes, carrots, celery, mushroom, and sugar.
Mix the corn flour and water to create an adhesive for the spring rolls.
Scoop a tablespoonful of the vegetable mixture into the middle of the spring roll sheets.
Brush the edges of the sheets with the corn flour adhesive and enclose around the filling to make spring rolls.
Preheat the air fryer to 204°C.
When warm, place the rolls inside and air fry for 15 minutes or until crisp.
Serve hot.

## Pesto Vegetable Skewers

**Prep time: 30 minutes | Cook time: 8 minutes | Makes 8 skewers**

1 medium courgette, trimmed and cut into ½-inch slices
½ medium brown onion, peeled and cut into 1-inch squares
1 medium red pepper, seeded and cut into 1-inch squares

16 whole cremini or chestnut mushrooms
80 ml basil pesto
½ teaspoon salt
¼ teaspoon ground black pepper

Divide courgette slices, onion, and pepper into eight even portions. Place on 6-inch skewers for a total of eight kebabs.
Add 2 mushrooms to each skewer and brush kebabs generously with pesto.
Sprinkle each kebab with salt and black pepper on all sides, then place into ungreased air fryer basket.
Adjust the temperature to 192°C and air fry for 8 minutes, turning kebabs halfway through cooking.
Vegetables will be browned at the edges and tender-crisp when done.
Serve warm.

## Cayenne Tahini Kale

**Prep time: 5 minutes | Cook time: 15 minutes | Serves 2 to 4**

Dressing:
60 ml tahini
60 ml fresh lemon juice
2 tablespoons olive oil
1 teaspoon sesame seeds
½ teaspoon garlic powder
¼ teaspoon cayenne pepper

Kale:
1 L packed torn kale leaves (stems and ribs removed and leaves torn into palm-size pieces)
Rock salt and freshly ground black pepper, to taste

Preheat the air fryer to 176°C.
Make the dressing: Whisk together the tahini, lemon juice, olive oil, sesame seeds, garlic powder, and cayenne pepper in a large bowl until well mixed.
Add the kale and massage the dressing thoroughly all over the leaves.
Sprinkle the salt and pepper to season.
Place the kale in the air fryer basket in a single layer and air fry for about 15 minutes, or until the leaves are slightly wilted and crispy.
Remove from the basket and serve on a plate.

# Chapter 4 Poultry

# Chapter 4 Poultry

## Stuffed Chicken Florentine

**Prep time: 10 minutes | Cook time: 20 minutes | Serves 4**

3 tablespoons pine nuts
40 g frozen spinach, thawed and squeezed dry
75 g ricotta cheese
2 tablespoons grated Parmesan cheese
3 cloves garlic, minced
Salt and freshly ground black pepper, to taste
4 small boneless, skinless chicken breast halves (about 680 g)
8 slices bacon

Place the pine nuts in a small pan and set in the air fryer basket. Set the air fryer to 200°C and air fry for 2 to 3 minutes until toasted. Remove the pine nuts to a mixing bowl and continue preheating the air fryer.
In a large bowl, combine the spinach, ricotta, Parmesan, and garlic. Season to taste with salt and pepper and stir well until thoroughly combined.
Using a sharp knife, cut into the chicken breasts, slicing them across and opening them up like a book, but be careful not to cut them all the way through. Sprinkle the chicken with salt and pepper. Spoon equal amounts of the spinach mixture into the chicken, then fold the top of the chicken breast back over the top of the stuffing. Wrap each chicken breast with 2 slices of bacon.
Working in batches if necessary, air fry the chicken for 18 to 20 minutes until the bacon is crisp and a thermometer inserted into the thickest part of the chicken registers 76°C.

## Bacon-Wrapped Chicken Breasts Rolls

**Prep time: 10 minutes | Cook time: 15 minutes | Serves 4**

15 g chopped fresh chives
2 tablespoons lemon juice
1 teaspoon dried sage
1 teaspoon fresh rosemary leaves
15 g fresh parsley leaves
4 cloves garlic, peeled
1 teaspoon ground fennel
3 teaspoons sea salt
½ teaspoon red pepper flakes
4 (115 g) boneless, skinless chicken breasts, pounded to ¼ inch thick
8 slices bacon
Sprigs of fresh rosemary, for garnish
Cooking spray

Preheat the air fryer to 170°C. Spritz the air fryer basket with cooking spray.
Put the chives, lemon juice, sage, rosemary, parsley, garlic, fennel, salt, and red pepper flakes in a food processor, then pulse to purée until smooth.
Unfold the chicken breasts on a clean work surface, then brush the top side of the chicken breasts with the sauce.
Roll the chicken breasts up from the shorter side, then wrap each chicken rolls with 2 bacon slices to cover. Secure with toothpicks.
Arrange the rolls in the preheated air fryer, then cook for 10 minutes. Flip the rolls halfway through.
Increase the heat to 200°C and air fry for 5 more minutes or until the bacon is browned and crispy.
Transfer the rolls to a large plate. Discard the toothpicks and spread with rosemary sprigs before serving.

## Easy Chicken Fingers

**Prep time: 20 minutes | Cook time: 30 minutes | Makes 12 chicken fingers**

60 g all-purpose flour
240 g panko breadcrumbs
2 tablespoons rapeseed oil
1 large egg
3 boneless and skinless chicken
breasts, each cut into 4 strips
Kosher salt and freshly ground black pepper, to taste
Cooking spray

Preheat the air fryer to 180°C. Spritz the air fryer basket with cooking spray.
Pour the flour in a large bowl. Combine the panko and rapeseed oil on a shallow dish. Whisk the egg in a separate bowl.
Rub the chicken strips with salt and ground black pepper on a clean work surface, then dip the chicken in the bowl of flour. Shake the excess off and dunk the chicken strips in the bowl of whisked egg, then roll the strips over the panko to coat well.
Arrange 4 strips in the air fryer basket each time and air fry for 10 minutes or until crunchy and lightly browned. Flip the strips halfway through. Repeat with remaining ingredients.
Serve immediately.

## Ham Chicken with Cheese

**Prep time: 15 minutes | Cook time: 25 minutes | Serves 4**

55 g unsalted butter, softened
115 g cream cheese, softened
1½ teaspoons Dijon mustard
2 tablespoons white wine vinegar
60 ml water
280 g shredded cooked chicken
115 g ham, chopped
115 g sliced Swiss or Provolone cheese

Preheat the air fryer to 190°C. Lightly coat a casserole dish that will fit in the air fryer, such as an 8-inch round pan, with olive oil and set aside.
In a large bowl and using an electric mixer, combine the butter, cream cheese, Dijon mustard, and vinegar. With the motor running at low speed, slowly add the water and beat until smooth. Set aside.
Arrange an even layer of chicken in the bottom of the prepared pan, followed by the ham. Spread the butter and cream cheese mixture on top of the ham, followed by the cheese slices on the top layer.
Air fry for 20 to 25 minutes until warmed through and the cheese has browned.

## Jalapeño Chicken Balls

### Prep time: 10 minutes | Cook time: 25 minutes | Serves 4

1 medium red onion, minced
2 garlic cloves, minced
1 jalapeño pepper, minced
2 teaspoons extra-virgin olive oil
3 tablespoons ground almonds
1 egg
1 teaspoon dried thyme
450 g chicken mince breast
Cooking oil spray

Insert the crisper plate into the basket and the basket into the unit. Preheat the unit by selecting BAKE, setting the temperature to 200°C, and setting the time to 3 minutes. Select START/STOP to begin.
In a 6-by-2-inch round pan, combine the red onion, garlic, jalapeño, and olive oil.
Once the unit is preheated, place the pan into the basket.
Select BAKE, set the temperature to 200°C, and set the time to 4 minutes. Select START/STOP to begin.
When the cooking is complete, the vegetables should be crisp-tender. Transfer to a medium bowl.
Mix the almonds, egg, and thyme into the vegetable mixture. Add the chicken and mix until just combined. Form the chicken mixture into about 24 (1-inch) balls.
Insert the crisper plate into the basket and the basket into the unit. Preheat the unit by selecting BAKE, setting the temperature to 200°C, and setting the time to 3 minutes. Select START/STOP to begin.
Once the unit is preheated, spray the crisper plate with cooking oil. Working in batches, place half the meatballs in a single layer, not touching, into the basket.
Select BAKE, set the temperature to 200°C, and set the time to 10 minutes. Select START/STOP to begin.1When the cooking is complete, a food thermometer inserted into the meatballs should register at least 76°C.1Repeat steps 8 and 9 with the remaining meatballs. Serve warm.

## Golden Chicken Cutlets

### Prep time: 15 minutes | Cook time: 15 minutes | Serves 4

2 tablespoons panko breadcrumbs
20 g grated Parmesan cheese
⅛ tablespoon paprika
½ tablespoon garlic powder
2 large eggs
4 chicken cutlets
1 tablespoon parsley
Salt and ground black pepper, to taste
Cooking spray

Preheat air fryer to 200°C. Spritz the air fryer basket with cooking spray.
Combine the breadcrumbs, Parmesan, paprika, garlic powder, salt, and ground black pepper in a large bowl. Stir to mix well. Beat the eggs in a separate bowl.
Dredge the chicken cutlets in the beaten eggs, then roll over the breadcrumbs mixture to coat well. Shake the excess off.
Transfer the chicken cutlets in the preheated air fryer and spritz with cooking spray.
Air fry for 15 minutes or until crispy and golden brown. Flip the cutlets halfway through.
Serve with parsley on top.

## Classic Whole Chicken

### Prep time: 5 minutes | Cook time: 50 minutes | Serves 4

Oil, for spraying
1 (1.8 kg) whole chicken, giblets removed
1 tablespoon olive oil
1 teaspoon paprika
½ teaspoon granulated garlic
½ teaspoon salt
½ teaspoon freshly ground black pepper
¼ teaspoon finely chopped fresh parsley, for garnish

Line the air fryer basket with parchment and spray lightly with oil. Pat the chicken dry with paper towels. Rub it with the olive oil until evenly coated.
In a small bowl, mix together the paprika, garlic, salt, and black pepper and sprinkle it evenly over the chicken.
Place the chicken in the prepared basket, breast-side down.
Air fry at 180°C for 30 minutes, flip, and cook for another 20 minutes, or until the internal temperature reaches 76°C and the juices run clear.
Sprinkle with the parsley before serving.
Crispy Duck with Cherry Sauce
Prep time: 10 minutes | Cook time: 33 minutes | Serves 2 to 4
1 whole duck (2.3 kg), split in half, back and rib bones removed

## 1 teaspoon olive oil

### Salt and freshly ground black pepper, to taste

Cherry Sauce:
1 tablespoon butter
1 shallot, minced
120 ml sherry
240 g cherry preserves
240 ml chicken stock
1 teaspoon white wine vinegar
1 teaspoon fresh thyme leaves
Salt and freshly ground black pepper, to taste

Preheat the air fryer to 200°C.
Trim some of the fat from the duck. Rub olive oil on the duck and season with salt and pepper. Place the duck halves in the air fryer basket, breast side up and facing the centre of the basket.
Air fry the duck for 20 minutes. Turn the duck over and air fry for another 6 minutes.
While duck is air frying, make the cherry sauce. Melt the butter in a large sauté pan. Add the shallot and sauté until it is just starting to brown, about 2 to 3 minutes. Add the sherry and deglaze the pan by scraping up any brown bits from the bottom of the pan. Simmer the liquid for a few minutes, until it has reduced by half. Add the cherry preserves, chicken stock and white wine vinegar. Whisk well to combine all the ingredients. Simmer the sauce until it thickens and coats the back of a spoon, about 5 to 7 minutes. Season with salt and pepper and stir in the fresh thyme leaves.
When the air fryer timer goes off, spoon some cherry sauce over the duck and continue to air fry at 200°C for 4 more minutes. Then, turn the duck halves back over so that the breast side is facing up. Spoon more cherry sauce over the top of the duck, covering the skin completely. Air fry for 3 more minutes and then remove the duck to a plate to rest for a few minutes.
Serve the duck in halves, or cut each piece in half again for a smaller serving. Spoon any additional sauce over the duck or serve it on the side.

## Classic Chicken Kebab

**Prep time: 35 minutes | Cook time: 25 minutes | Serves 4**

| | |
|---|---|
| 60 ml olive oil | 450 g boneless skinless chicken |
| 1 teaspoon garlic powder | thighs, cut into 1-inch pieces |
| 1 teaspoon onion powder | 1 red bell pepper, cut into 1-inch |
| 1 teaspoon ground cumin | pieces |
| ½ teaspoon dried oregano | 1 red onion, cut into 1-inch |
| ½ teaspoon dried basil | pieces |
| 60 ml lemon juice | 1 courgette, cut into 1-inch |
| 1 tablespoon apple cider vinegar | pieces |
| Olive oil cooking spray | 12 cherry tomatoes |

In a large bowl, mix together the olive oil, garlic powder, onion powder, cumin, oregano, basil, lemon juice, and apple cider vinegar.

Spray six skewers with olive oil cooking spray.

On each skewer, slide on a piece of chicken, then a piece of bell pepper, onion, courgette, and finally a tomato and then repeat. Each skewer should have at least two pieces of each item.

Once all of the skewers are prepared, place them in a 9-by-13-inch baking dish and pour the olive oil marinade over the top of the skewers. Turn each skewer so that all sides of the chicken and vegetables are coated.

Cover the dish with plastic wrap and place it in the refrigerator for 30 minutes.

After 30 minutes, preheat the air fryer to 192ºC. (If using a grill attachment, make sure it is inside the air fryer during preheating.)

Remove the skewers from the marinade and lay them in a single layer in the air fryer basket. If the air fryer has a grill attachment, you can also lay them on this instead.

Cook for 10 minutes. Rotate the kebabs, then cook them for 15 minutes more.

Remove the skewers from the air fryer and let them rest for 5 minutes before serving.

## Sriracha-Honey Chicken Nuggets

**Prep time: 15 minutes | Cook time: 19 minutes | Serves 6**

| | |
|---|---|
| Oil, for spraying | ½ teaspoon freshly ground black |
| 1 large egg | pepper |
| 180 ml milk | 2 boneless, skinless chicken |
| 125 g all-purpose flour | breasts, cut into bite-size pieces |
| 2 tablespoons icing sugar | 140 g barbecue sauce |
| ½ teaspoon paprika | 2 tablespoons honey |
| ½ teaspoon salt | 1 tablespoon Sriracha |

Line the air fryer basket with parchment and spray lightly with oil.

In a small bowl, whisk together the egg and milk.

In a medium bowl, combine the flour, icing sugar, paprika, salt, and black pepper and stir.

Coat the chicken in the egg mixture, then dredge in the flour mixture until evenly coated.

Place the chicken in the prepared basket and spray liberally with oil.

Air fry at 200ºC for 8 minutes, flip, spray with more oil, and cook for another 6 to 8 minutes, or until the internal temperature reaches 76ºC and the juices run clear.

In a large bowl, mix together the barbecue sauce, honey, and Sriracha.

Transfer the chicken to the bowl and toss until well coated with the barbecue sauce mixture.

Line the air fryer basket with fresh parchment, return the chicken to the basket, and cook for another 2 to 3 minutes, until browned and crispy.

## Ginger Turmeric Chicken Thighs

**Prep time: 5 minutes | Cook time: 25 minutes | Serves 4**

| | |
|---|---|
| 4 (115 g) boneless, skin-on | ½ teaspoon salt |
| chicken thighs | ½ teaspoon garlic powder |
| 2 tablespoons coconut oil, | ½ teaspoon ground ginger |
| melted | ¼ teaspoon ground black pepper |
| ½ teaspoon ground turmeric | |

Place chicken thighs in a large bowl and drizzle with coconut oil. Sprinkle with remaining ingredients and toss to coat both sides of thighs.

Place thighs skin side up into ungreased air fryer basket. Adjust the temperature to 200ºC and air fry for 25 minutes. After 10 minutes, turn thighs. When 5 minutes remain, flip thighs once more. Chicken will be done when skin is golden brown and the internal temperature is at least 76ºC.

Serve warm.

## Peanut Butter Chicken Satay

**Prep time: 12 minutes | Cook time: 12 to 18 minutes | Serves 4**

| | |
|---|---|
| 120 g crunchy peanut butter | 2 garlic cloves, minced |
| 80 ml chicken broth | 2 tablespoons extra-virgin olive |
| 3 tablespoons low-sodium soy | oil |
| sauce | 1 teaspoon curry powder |
| 2 tablespoons freshly squeezed | 450 g chicken tenders |
| lemon juice | Cooking oil spray |

In a medium bowl, whisk the peanut butter, broth, soy sauce, lemon juice, garlic, olive oil, and curry powder until smooth.

Place 2 tablespoons of this mixture into a small bowl. Transfer the remaining sauce to a serving bowl and set aside.

Add the chicken tenders to the bowl with the 2 tablespoons of sauce and stir to coat. Let stand for a few minutes to marinate.

Insert the crisper plate into the basket and the basket into the unit. Preheat the unit by selecting AIR FRY, setting the temperature to 200ºC, and setting the time to 3 minutes. Select START/STOP to begin.

Run a 6-inch bamboo skewer lengthwise through each chicken tender.

Once the unit is preheated, spray the crisper plate with cooking oil. Working in batches, place half the chicken skewers into the basket in a single layer without overlapping.

Select AIR FRY, set the temperature to 200ºC, and set the time to 9 minutes. Select START/STOP to begin.

After 6 minutes, check the chicken. If a food thermometer inserted into the chicken registers 76ºC, it is done. If not, resume cooking.

Repeat steps 6, 7, and 8 with the remaining chicken.1When the cooking is complete, serve the chicken with the reserved sauce.

# Mediterranean Stuffed Chicken Breasts

**Prep time: 5 minutes | Cook time: 20 to 25 minutes | Serves 4**

| | |
|---|---|
| 4 small boneless, skinless chicken breast halves (about 680 g) | Zest of ½ lemon |
| Salt and freshly ground black pepper, to taste | 1 teaspoon minced fresh rosemary or ½ teaspoon ground dried rosemary |
| 115 g goat cheese | 50 g almond meal |
| 6 pitted Kalamata olives, coarsely chopped | 60 ml balsamic vinegar |
| | 6 tablespoons unsalted butter |

Preheat the air fryer to 180ºC.

With a boning knife, cut a wide pocket into the thickest part of each chicken breast half, taking care not to cut all the way through. Season the chicken evenly on both sides with salt and freshly ground black pepper.

In a small bowl, mix the cheese, olives, lemon zest, and rosemary. Stuff the pockets with the cheese mixture and secure with toothpicks.

Place the almond meal in a shallow bowl and dredge the chicken, shaking off the excess. Coat lightly with olive oil spray.

Working in batches if necessary, arrange the chicken breasts in a single layer in the air fryer basket. Pausing halfway through the cooking time to flip the chicken, air fry for 20 to 25 minutes, until a thermometer inserted into the thickest part registers 76ºC.

While the chicken is baking, prepare the sauce. In a small pan over medium heat, simmer the balsamic vinegar until thick and syrupy, about 5 minutes. Set aside until the chicken is done. When ready to serve, warm the sauce over medium heat and whisk in the butter, 1 tablespoon at a time, until melted and smooth. Season to taste with salt and pepper.

Serve the chicken breasts with the sauce drizzled on top.

# Buttermilk-Fried Drumsticks

**Prep time: 10 minutes | Cook time: 25 minutes | Serves 2**

| | |
|---|---|
| 1 egg | 1 teaspoon salt |
| 120 g buttermilk | ¼ teaspoon ground black pepper (to mix into coating) |
| 90 g self-rising flour | |
| 90 g seasoned panko bread crumbs | 4 chicken drumsticks, skin on |
| | Oil for misting or cooking spray |

Beat together egg and buttermilk in shallow dish.

In a second shallow dish, combine the flour, panko crumbs, salt, and pepper.

Sprinkle chicken legs with additional salt and pepper to taste.

Dip legs in buttermilk mixture, then roll in panko mixture, pressing in crumbs to make coating stick. Mist with oil or cooking spray.

Spray the air fryer basket with cooking spray.

Cook drumsticks at 180ºC for 10 minutes. Turn pieces over and cook an additional 10 minutes.

Turn pieces to check for browning. If you have any white spots that haven't begun to brown, spritz them with oil or cooking spray. Continue cooking for 5 more minutes or until crust is golden brown and juices run clear. Larger, meatier drumsticks will take longer to cook than small ones.

# Buffalo Chicken Cheese Sticks

**Prep time: 5 minutes | Cook time: 8 minutes | Serves 2**

| | |
|---|---|
| 140 g shredded cooked chicken | cheese |
| 60 ml buffalo sauce | 1 large egg |
| 220 g shredded Mozzarella | 55 g crumbled feta |

In a large bowl, mix all ingredients except the feta. Cut a piece of parchment to fit your air fryer basket and press the mixture into a ½-inch-thick circle.

Sprinkle the mixture with feta and place into the air fryer basket.

Adjust the temperature to 200ºC and air fry for 8 minutes.

After 5 minutes, flip over the cheese mixture.

Allow to cool 5 minutes before cutting into sticks. Serve warm.

# Cracked-Pepper Chicken Wings

**Prep time: 15 minutes | Cook time: 20 minutes | Serves 4**

| | |
|---|---|
| 450 g chicken wings | ½ teaspoon garlic powder |
| 3 tablespoons vegetable oil | ½ teaspoon kosher salt |
| 60 g all-purpose flour | 1½ teaspoons freshly cracked black pepper |
| ½ teaspoon smoked paprika | |

Place the chicken wings in a large bowl. Drizzle the vegetable oil over wings and toss to coat.

In a separate bowl, whisk together the flour, paprika, garlic powder, salt, and pepper until combined.

Dredge the wings in the flour mixture one at a time, coating them well, and place in the air fryer basket. Set the air fryer to 200ºC for 20 minutes, turning the wings halfway through the cooking time, until the breading is browned and crunchy.

# Yellow Curry Chicken Thighs with Peanuts

**Prep time: 10 minutes | Cook time: 20 minutes | Serves 6**

| | |
|---|---|
| 120 ml unsweetened full-fat coconut milk | 1 tablespoon minced garlic |
| 2 tablespoons yellow curry paste | 1 teaspoon kosher salt |
| | 450 g boneless, skinless chicken thighs, halved crosswise |
| 1 tablespoon minced fresh ginger | 2 tablespoons chopped peanuts |

In a large bowl, stir together the coconut milk, curry paste, ginger, garlic, and salt until well blended. Add the chicken; toss well to coat. Marinate at room temperature for 30 minutes, or cover and refrigerate for up to 24 hours.

Preheat the air fryer to 190ºC.

Place the chicken (along with marinade) in a baking pan. Place the pan in the air fryer basket. Bake for 20 minutes, turning the chicken halfway through the cooking time. Use a meat thermometer to ensure the chicken has reached an internal temperature of 76ºC.

Sprinkle the chicken with the chopped peanuts and serve.

# Chicken Thighs in Waffles

**Prep time: 1 hour 20 minutes | Cook time: 40 minutes | Serves 4**

For the chicken:
4 chicken thighs, skin on
240 ml low-fat buttermilk
65 g all-purpose flour
½ teaspoon garlic powder
½ teaspoon mustard powder
1 teaspoon kosher salt
½ teaspoon freshly ground black pepper
85 g honey, for serving

Cooking spray
For the waffles:
65 g all-purpose flour
65 g whole wheat pastry flour
1 large egg, beaten
240 ml low-fat buttermilk
1 teaspoon baking powder
2 tablespoons rapeseed oil
½ teaspoon kosher salt
1 tablespoon granulated sugar

Combine the chicken thighs with buttermilk in a large bowl. Wrap the bowl in plastic and refrigerate to marinate for at least an hour.
Preheat the air fryer to 180ºC. Spritz the air fryer basket with cooking spray.
Combine the flour, mustard powder, garlic powder, salt, and black pepper in a shallow dish. Stir to mix well.
Remove the thighs from the buttermilk and pat dry with paper towels. Sit the bowl of buttermilk aside.
Dip the thighs in the flour mixture first, then into the buttermilk, and then into the flour mixture. Shake the excess off.
Arrange 2 thighs in the preheated air fryer and spritz with cooking spray. Air fryer for 20 minutes or until an instant-read thermometer inserted in the thickest part of the chicken thighs registers at least 76ºC. Flip the thighs halfway through. Repeat with remaining thighs.
Meanwhile, make the waffles: combine the ingredients for the waffles in a large bowl. Stir to mix well, then arrange the mixture in a waffle iron and cook until a golden and fragrant waffle forms.
Remove the waffles from the waffle iron and slice into 4 pieces. Remove the chicken thighs from the air fryer and allow to cool for 5 minutes.
Arrange each chicken thigh on each waffle piece and drizzle with 1 tablespoon of honey. Serve warm.

# Lemon-Dijon Boneless Chicken

**Prep time: 30 minutes | Cook time: 13 to 16 minutes | Serves 6**

115 g sugar-free mayonnaise
1 tablespoon Dijon mustard
1 tablespoon freshly squeezed lemon juice (optional)
1 tablespoon coconut aminos
1 teaspoon Italian seasoning

1 teaspoon sea salt
½ teaspoon freshly ground black pepper
¼ teaspoon cayenne pepper
680 g boneless, skinless chicken breasts or thighs

In a small bowl, combine the mayonnaise, mustard, lemon juice (if using), coconut aminos, Italian seasoning, salt, black pepper, and cayenne pepper.
Place the chicken in a shallow dish or large zip-top plastic bag. Add the marinade, making sure all the pieces are coated. Cover and refrigerate for at least 30 minutes or up to 4 hours.
Set the air fryer to 200ºC. Arrange the chicken in a single layer in the air fryer basket, working in batches if necessary. Air fry for 7 minutes. Flip the chicken and continue cooking for 6 to 9 minutes more, until an instant-read thermometer reads 70ºC.

# Chicken Pesto Parmigiana

**Prep time: 10 minutes | Cook time: 23 minutes | Serves 4**

2 large eggs
1 tablespoon water
Fine sea salt and ground black pepper, to taste
85 g powdered Parmesan cheese
2 teaspoons Italian seasoning
4 (140 g) boneless, skinless chicken breasts or thighs,

pounded to ¼ inch thick
65 g pesto
115 g shredded Mozzarella cheese
Finely chopped fresh basil, for garnish (optional)
Grape tomatoes, halved, for serving (optional)

Spray the air fryer basket with avocado oil. Preheat the air fryer to 200ºC.
Crack the eggs into a shallow baking dish, add the water and a pinch each of salt and pepper, and whisk to combine. In another shallow baking dish, stir together the Parmesan and Italian seasoning until well combined.
Season the chicken breasts well on both sides with salt and pepper. Dip one chicken breast in the eggs and let any excess drip off, then dredge both sides of the breast in the Parmesan mixture.
Spray the breast with avocado oil and place it in the air fryer basket. Repeat with the remaining 3 chicken breasts.
Air fry the chicken in the air fryer for 20 minutes, or until the internal temperature reaches 76ºC and the breading is golden brown, flipping halfway through.
Dollop each chicken breast with ¼ of the pesto and top with the Mozzarella. Return the breasts to the air fryer and cook for 3 minutes, or until the cheese is melted. Garnish with basil and serve with halved grape tomatoes on the side, if desired.
Store leftovers in an airtight container in the refrigerator for up to 4 days. Reheat in a preheated 200ºC air fryer for 5 minutes, or until warmed through.

# Lemon Thyme Roasted Chicken

**Prep time: 10 minutes | Cook time: 60 minutes | Serves 6**

2 tablespoons baking powder
1 teaspoon smoked paprika
Sea salt and freshly ground black pepper, to taste
900 g chicken wings or chicken drumettes
Avocado oil spray

80 ml avocado oil
120 ml Buffalo hot sauce, such as Frank's RedHot
4 tablespoons unsalted butter
2 tablespoons apple cider vinegar
1 teaspoon minced garlic

In a large bowl, stir together the baking powder, smoked paprika, and salt and pepper to taste. Add the chicken wings and toss to coat. Set the air fryer to 200ºC. Spray the wings with oil.
Place the wings in the basket in a single layer, working in batches, and air fry for 20 to 25 minutes. Check with an instant-read thermometer and remove when they reach 70ºC. Let rest until they reach 76ºC.
While the wings are cooking, whisk together the avocado oil, hot sauce, butter, vinegar, and garlic in a small saucepan over medium-low heat until warm.
When the wings are done cooking, toss them with the Buffalo sauce. Serve warm.

## Sweet Chili Spiced Chicken

### Prep time: 10 minutes | Cook time: 43 minutes | Serves 4

Spice Rub:
2 tablespoons brown sugar
2 tablespoons paprika
1 teaspoon dry mustard powder
1 teaspoon chili powder
2 tablespoons coarse sea salt or

kosher salt
2 teaspoons coarsely ground black pepper
1 tablespoon vegetable oil
1 (1.6 kg) chicken, cut into 8 pieces

Prepare the spice rub by combining the brown sugar, paprika, mustard powder, chili powder, salt and pepper. Rub the oil all over the chicken pieces and then rub the spice mix onto the chicken, covering completely. This is done very easily in a zipper sealable bag. You can do this ahead of time and let the chicken marinate in the refrigerator, or just proceed with cooking right away.
Preheat the air fryer to 190ºC.
Air fry the chicken in two batches. Place the two chicken thighs and two drumsticks into the air fryer basket. Air fry at 190ºC for 10 minutes. Then, gently turn the chicken pieces over and air fry for another 10 minutes. Remove the chicken pieces and let them rest on a plate while you cook the chicken breasts. Air fry the chicken breasts, skin side down for 8 minutes. Turn the chicken breasts over and air fry for another 12 minutes.
Lower the temperature of the air fryer to 170ºC. Place the first batch of chicken on top of the second batch already in the basket and air fry for a final 3 minutes.
Let the chicken rest for 5 minutes and serve warm with some mashed potatoes and a green salad or vegetables.

## Spicy Chicken Thighs and Gold Potatoes

### Prep time: 5 minutes | Cook time: 25 minutes | Serves 4

4 bone-in, skin-on chicken thighs
½ teaspoon kosher salt or ¼ teaspoon fine salt
2 tablespoons melted unsalted butter
2 teaspoons Worcestershire sauce
2 teaspoons curry powder
1 teaspoon dried oregano leaves

½ teaspoon dry mustard
½ teaspoon granulated garlic
¼ teaspoon paprika
¼ teaspoon hot pepper sauce
Cooking oil spray
4 medium Yukon gold potatoes, chopped
1 tablespoon extra-virgin olive oil

Sprinkle the chicken thighs on both sides with salt.
In a medium bowl, stir together the melted butter, Worcestershire sauce, curry powder, oregano, dry mustard, granulated garlic, paprika, and hot pepper sauce. Add the thighs to the sauce and stir to coat.
Insert the crisper plate into the basket and the basket into the unit. Preheat the unit by selecting AIR FRY, setting the temperature to 200ºC, and setting the time to 3 minutes. Select START/STOP to begin.
Once the unit is preheated, spray the crisper plate with cooking oil. In the basket, combine the potatoes and olive oil and toss to coat.
Add the wire rack to the air fryer and place the chicken thighs on top.
Select AIR FRY, set the temperature to 200ºC, and set the time to

25 minutes. Select START/STOP to begin.
After 19 minutes check the chicken thighs. If a food thermometer inserted into the chicken registers 76ºC, transfer them to a clean plate, and cover with aluminum foil to keep warm. If they aren't cooked to 76ºC, resume cooking for another 1 to 2 minutes until they are done. Remove them from the unit along with the rack.
Remove the basket and shake it to distribute the potatoes. Reinsert the basket to resume cooking for 3 to 6 minutes, or until the potatoes are crisp and golden brown.
When the cooking is complete, serve the chicken with the potatoes.

## Apricot-Glazed Turkey Tenderloin

### Prep time: 20 minutes | Cook time: 30 minutes | Serves 4

Olive oil
80 g sugar-free apricot preserves
½ tablespoon spicy brown mustard

680 g turkey breast tenderloin
Salt and freshly ground black pepper, to taste

Spray the air fryer basket lightly with olive oil.
In a small bowl, combine the apricot preserves and mustard to make a paste.
Season the turkey with salt and pepper. Spread the apricot paste all over the turkey.
Place the turkey in the air fryer basket and lightly spray with olive oil.
Air fry at 190ºC for 15 minutes. Flip the turkey over and lightly spray with olive oil. Air fry until the internal temperature reaches at least 80ºC, an additional 10 to 15 minutes.
Let the turkey rest for 10 minutes before slicing and serving.

## Chicken Schnitzel

### Prep time: 15 minutes | Cook time: 5 minutes | Serves 4

60 g all-purpose flour
1 teaspoon marjoram
½ teaspoon thyme
1 teaspoon dried parsley flakes
½ teaspoon salt
1 egg

1 teaspoon lemon juice
1 teaspoon water
120 g breadcrumbs
4 chicken tenders, pounded thin, cut in half lengthwise
Cooking spray

Preheat the air fryer to 200ºC and spritz with cooking spray.
Combine the flour, marjoram, thyme, parsley, and salt in a shallow dish. Stir to mix well.
Whisk the egg with lemon juice and water in a large bowl. Pour the breadcrumbs in a separate shallow dish.
Roll the chicken halves in the flour mixture first, then in the egg mixture, and then roll over the breadcrumbs to coat well. Shake the excess off.
Arrange the chicken halves in the preheated air fryer and spritz with cooking spray on both sides.
Air fry for 5 minutes or until the chicken halves are golden brown and crispy. Flip the halves halfway through.
Serve immediately.

## Chipotle Drumsticks

**Prep time: 15 minutes | Cook time: 20 minutes | Serves 4**

1 tablespoon tomato paste
½ teaspoon chipotle powder
¼ teaspoon apple cider vinegar
¼ teaspoon garlic powder
8 chicken drumsticks
½ teaspoon salt
⅛ teaspoon ground black pepper

In a small bowl, combine tomato paste, chipotle powder, vinegar, and garlic powder.
Sprinkle drumsticks with salt and pepper, then place into a large bowl and pour in tomato paste mixture. Toss or stir to evenly coat all drumsticks in mixture.
Place drumsticks into ungreased air fryer basket. Adjust the temperature to 200ºC and air fry for 25 minutes, turning drumsticks halfway through cooking. Drumsticks will be dark red with an internal temperature of at least 76ºC when done. Serve warm.

## Thai-Style Cornish Game Hens

**Prep time: 30 minutes | Cook time: 20 minutes | Serves 4**

20 g chopped fresh coriander leaves and stems
60 ml fish sauce
1 tablespoon soy sauce
1 serrano chili, seeded and chopped
8 garlic cloves, smashed
2 tablespoons sugar
2 tablespoons lemongrass paste
2 teaspoons black pepper
2 teaspoons ground coriander
1 teaspoon kosher salt
1 teaspoon ground turmeric
2 Cornish game hens, giblets removed, split in half lengthwise

In a blender, combine the coriander, fish sauce, soy sauce, serrano, garlic, sugar, lemongrass, black pepper, coriander, salt, and turmeric. Blend until smooth.
Place the game hen halves in a large bowl. Pour the coriander mixture over the hen halves and toss to coat. Marinate at room temperature for 30 minutes, or cover and refrigerate for up to 24 hours.
Arrange the hen halves in a single layer in the air fryer basket. Set the air fryer to 200ºC for 20 minutes. Use a meat thermometer to ensure the game hens have reached an internal temperature of 76ºC.

## Cheesy Pepperoni and Chicken Pizza

**Prep time: 15 minutes | Cook time: 15 minutes | Serves 6**

280 g cooked chicken, cubed
240 g pizza sauce
20 slices pepperoni
20 g grated Parmesan cheese
225 g shredded Mozzarella cheese
Cooking spray

Preheat the air fryer to 190ºC. Spritz a baking pan with cooking spray.
Arrange the chicken cubes in the prepared baking pan, then top the cubes with pizza sauce and pepperoni. Stir to coat the cubes and pepperoni with sauce.
Scatter the cheeses on top, then place the baking pan in the preheated air fryer. Air fryer for 15 minutes or until frothy and the cheeses melt.
Serve immediately.

## Herbed Turkey Breast with Simple Dijon Sauce

**Prep time: 5 minutes | Cook time: 30 minutes | Serves 4**

1 teaspoon chopped fresh sage
1 teaspoon chopped fresh tarragon
1 teaspoon chopped fresh thyme leaves
1 teaspoon chopped fresh rosemary leaves
1½ teaspoons sea salt
1 teaspoon ground black pepper
1 (900 g) turkey breast
3 tablespoons Dijon mustard
3 tablespoons butter, melted
Cooking spray

Preheat the air fryer to 200ºC. Spritz the air fryer basket with cooking spray.
Combine the herbs, salt, and black pepper in a small bowl. Stir to mix well. Set aside.
Combine the Dijon mustard and butter in a separate bowl. Stir to mix well.
Rub the turkey with the herb mixture on a clean work surface, then brush the turkey with Dijon mixture.
Arrange the turkey in the preheated air fryer basket. Air fry for 30 minutes or until an instant-read thermometer inserted in the thickest part of the turkey breast reaches at least 76ºC.
Transfer the cooked turkey breast on a large plate and slice to serve.

## Chicken and Avocado Fajitas

**Prep time: 10 minutes | Cook time: 10 to 14 minutes | Serves 4**

Cooking oil spray
4 boneless, skinless chicken breasts, sliced crosswise
1 small red onion, sliced
2 red bell peppers, seeded and sliced
120 ml spicy ranch salad
dressing, divided
½ teaspoon dried oregano
8 corn tortillas
40 g torn butter lettuce leaves
2 avocados, peeled, pitted, and chopped

Insert the crisper plate into the basket and the basket into the unit. Preheat the unit by selecting BAKE, setting the temperature to 190ºC, and setting the time to 3 minutes. Select START/STOP to begin.
Once the unit is preheated, spray the crisper plate with cooking oil. Place the chicken, red onion, and red bell pepper into the basket. Drizzle with 1 tablespoon of the salad dressing and season with the oregano. Toss to combine.
Select BAKE, set the temperature to 190ºC, and set the time to 14 minutes. Select START/STOP to begin.
After 10 minutes, check the chicken. If a food thermometer inserted into the chicken registers at least 76ºC, it is done. If not, resume cooking.
When the cooking is complete, transfer the chicken and vegetables to a bowl and toss with the remaining salad dressing.
Serve the chicken mixture family-style with the tortillas, lettuce, and avocados, and let everyone make their own plates.

# Chicken Breasts with Asparagus, Beans, and Rocket

**Prep time: 20 minutes | Cook time: 25 minutes | Serves 2**

160 g canned cannellini beans, rinsed
1½ tablespoons red wine vinegar
1 garlic clove, minced
2 tablespoons extra-virgin olive oil, divided
Salt and ground black pepper, to taste
½ red onion, sliced thinly
230 g asparagus, trimmed and cut into 1-inch lengths
2 (230 g) boneless, skinless chicken breasts, trimmed
¼ teaspoon paprika
½ teaspoon ground coriander
60 g baby rocket, rinsed and drained

Preheat the air fryer to 200°C.
Warm the beans in microwave for 1 minutes and combine with red wine vinegar, garlic, 1 tablespoon of olive oil, ¼ teaspoon of salt, and ¼ teaspoon of ground black pepper in a bowl. Stir to mix well.
Combine the onion with ⅛ teaspoon of salt, ⅛ teaspoon of ground black pepper, and 2 teaspoons of olive oil in a separate bowl. Toss to coat well.
Place the onion in the air fryer and air fry for 2 minutes, then add the asparagus and air fry for 8 more minutes or until the asparagus is tender. Shake the basket halfway through. Transfer the onion and asparagus to the bowl with beans. Set aside.
Toss the chicken breasts with remaining ingredients, except for the baby rocket, in a large bowl.
Put the chicken breasts in the air fryer and air fry for 14 minutes or until the internal temperature of the chicken reaches at least 76°C. Flip the breasts halfway through.
Remove the chicken from the air fryer and serve on an aluminum foil with asparagus, beans, onion, and rocket. Sprinkle with salt and ground black pepper. Toss to serve.

# Easy Chicken Nachos

**Prep time: 5 minutes | Cook time: 5 minutes | Serves 8**

Oil, for spraying
420 g shredded cooked chicken
1 (30 g) package ranch seasoning
60 g sour cream
55 g corn tortilla chips
75 g bacon bits
235 g shredded Cheddar cheese
1 tablespoon chopped spring onions

Line the air fryer basket with parchment and spray lightly with oil.
In a small bowl, mix together the chicken, ranch seasoning, and sour cream.
Place the tortilla chips in the prepared basket and top with the chicken mixture. Add the bacon bits, Cheddar cheese, and spring onions.
Air fry at 220°C for 3 to 5 minutes, or until heated through and the cheese is melted.

# Chicken Burgers with Ham and Cheese

**Prep time: 12 minutes | Cook time: 13 to 16 minutes | Serves 4**

40 g soft bread crumbs
3 tablespoons milk
1 egg, beaten
½ teaspoon dried thyme
Pinch salt
Freshly ground black pepper, to taste
570 g chicken mince
70 g finely chopped ham
75 g grated Gouda cheese
Olive oil for misting

Preheat the air fryer to 180°C.
In a medium bowl, combine the bread crumbs, milk, egg, thyme, salt, and pepper. Add the chicken and mix gently but thoroughly with clean hands.
Form the chicken into eight thin patties and place on waxed paper. Top four of the patties with the ham and cheese. Top with remaining four patties and gently press the edges together to seal, so the ham and cheese mixture is in the middle of the burger.
Place the burgers in the basket and mist with olive oil. Bake for 13 to 16 minutes or until the chicken is thoroughly cooked to 76°C as measured with a meat thermometer. Serve immediately.

# Chicken Shawarma

**Prep time: 30 minutes | Cook time: 15 minutes | Serves 4**

Shawarma Spice:
2 teaspoons dried oregano
1 teaspoon ground cinnamon
1 teaspoon ground cumin
1 teaspoon ground coriander
1 teaspoon kosher salt
½ teaspoon ground allspice
½ teaspoon cayenne pepper
Chicken:
450 g boneless, skinless chicken thighs, cut into large bite-size chunks
2 tablespoons vegetable oil
For Serving:
Tzatziki
Pita bread

For the shawarma spice: In a small bowl, combine the oregano, cayenne, cumin, coriander, salt, cinnamon, and allspice.
For the chicken: In a large bowl, toss together the chicken, vegetable oil, and shawarma spice to coat. Marinate at room temperature for 30 minutes or cover and refrigerate for up to 24 hours.
Place the chicken in the air fryer basket. Set the air fryer to 180°C for 15 minutes, or until the chicken reaches an internal temperature of 76°C.
Transfer the chicken to a serving platter. Serve with tzatziki and pita bread.

# One-Dish Chicken and Rice

**Prep time: 10 minutes | Cook time: 40 minutes | Serves 4**

190 g long-grain white rice, rinsed and drained
120 g cut frozen green beans (do not thaw)
1 tablespoon minced fresh ginger
3 cloves garlic, minced

1 tablespoon toasted sesame oil
1 teaspoon kosher salt
1 teaspoon black pepper
450 g chicken wings, preferably drumettes

In a baking pan, combine the rice, green beans, ginger, garlic, sesame oil, salt, and pepper. Stir to combine. Place the chicken wings on top of the rice mixture.

Cover the pan with foil. Make a long slash in the foil to allow the pan to vent steam. Place the pan in the air fryer basket. Set the air fryer to (190°C for 30 minutes.

Remove the foil. Set the air fryer to 200°C for 10 minutes, or until the wings have browned and rendered fat into the rice and vegetables, turning the wings halfway through the cooking time.

# Chapter 5 Beef, Pork, and Lamb

# Chapter 5 Beef, Pork, and Lamb

## Chicken-Fried Steak

**Prep time: 20 minutes | Cook time: 14 minutes | Serves 2**

Steak:
Oil, for spraying
180 ml all-purpose flour
1 teaspoon salt
1 teaspoon freshly ground black pepper
½ teaspoon paprika
½ teaspoon onion granules
1 teaspoon granulated garlic
180 ml buttermilk
½ teaspoon hot sauce
2 (140 g) minute steaks
Gravy:
2 tablespoons unsalted butter
2 tablespoons all-purpose flour
235 ml milk
½ teaspoon salt
½ teaspoon freshly ground black pepper

Make the Steak
Line the air fryer basket with parchment and spray lightly with oil.
In a medium bowl, mix together the flour, salt, black pepper, paprika, onion granules, and garlic.
In another bowl, whisk together the buttermilk and hot sauce.
Dredge the steaks in the flour mixture, dip in the buttermilk mixture, and dredge again in the flour until completely coated. Shake off any excess flour.
Place the steaks in the prepared basket and spray liberally with oil.
Air fry at 204ºC for 7 minutes, flip, spray with oil, and cook for another 6 to 7 minutes, or until crispy and browned.
Make the Gravy
In a small saucepan, whisk together the butter and flour over medium heat until the butter is melted. Slowly add the milk, salt, and black pepper, increase the heat to medium-high, and continue to cook, stirring constantly, until the mixture thickens. Remove from the heat.
Transfer the steaks to plates and pour the gravy over the top. Serve immediately.

## Smoky Pork Tenderloin

**Prep time: 5 minutes | Cook time: 19 to 22 minutes | Serves 6**

680 g pork tenderloin
1 tablespoon avocado oil
1 teaspoon chili powder
1 teaspoon smoked paprika
1 teaspoon garlic powder
1 teaspoon sea salt
1 teaspoon freshly ground black pepper

Pierce the tenderloin all over with a fork and rub the oil all over the meat.
In a small dish, stir together the chili powder, smoked paprika, garlic powder, salt, and pepper.
Rub the spice mixture all over the tenderloin.
Set the air fryer to 204ºC. Place the pork in the air fryer basket and air fry for 10 minutes. Flip the tenderloin and cook for 9 to 12 minutes more, until an instant-read thermometer reads at least 64ºC. Allow the tenderloin to rest for 5 minutes, then slice and serve.

## Greek Lamb Pitta Pockets

**Prep time: 15 minutes | Cook time: 6 minutes | Serves 4**

Dressing:
235 ml plain yogurt
1 tablespoon lemon juice
1 teaspoon dried dill, crushed
1 teaspoon ground oregano
½ teaspoon salt
Meatballs:
230 g lamb mince
1 tablespoon diced onion
1 teaspoon dried parsley
1 teaspoon dried dill, crushed
¼ teaspoon oregano
¼ teaspoon coriander
¼ teaspoon ground cumin
¼ teaspoon salt
4 pitta halves
Suggested Toppings:
1 red onion, slivered
1 medium cucumber, deseeded, thinly sliced
Crumbled feta cheese
Sliced black olives
Chopped fresh peppers

Preheat the air fryer to 200ºC.
Stir the dressing ingredients together in a small bowl and refrigerate while preparing lamb.
Combine all meatball ingredients in a large bowl and stir to distribute seasonings.
Shape meat mixture into 12 small meatballs, rounded or slightly flattened if you prefer.
Transfer the meatballs in the preheated air fryer and air fry for 6 minutes, until well done. Remove and drain on paper towels.
To serve, pile meatballs and the choice of toppings in pitta pockets and drizzle with dressing.

## Beef Whirls

**Prep time: 30 minutes | Cook time: 18 minutes | Serves 6**

3 minute steaks (170 g each)
1 (450 g) bottle Italian dressing
235 ml Italian-style bread crumbs (or plain bread crumbs with Italian seasoning to taste)
120 ml grated Parmesan cheese
1 teaspoon dried basil
1 teaspoon dried oregano
1 teaspoon dried parsley
60 ml beef stock
1 to 2 tablespoons oil

In a large resealable bag, combine the steaks and Italian dressing. Seal the bag and refrigerate to marinate for 2 hours.
In a medium bowl, whisk the bread crumbs, cheese, basil, oregano, and parsley until blended. Stir in the beef stock.
Place the steaks on a cutting board and cut each in half so you have 6 equal pieces. Sprinkle with the bread crumb mixture. Roll up the steaks, jelly roll-style, and secure with toothpicks.
Preheat the air fryer to 204ºC.
Place 3 roll-ups in the air fryer basket.
Cook for 5 minutes. Flip the roll-ups and spritz with oil. Cook for 4 minutes more until the internal temperature reaches 64ºC. Repeat with the remaining roll-ups. Let rest for 5 to 10 minutes before serving.

## Sesame Beef Lettuce Tacos

### Prep time: 30 minutes | Cook time: 8 to 10 minutes | Serves 4

| | |
|---|---|
| 60 ml soy sauce or tamari | 450 g bavette or skirt steak |
| 60 ml avocado oil | 8 butterhead lettuce leaves |
| 2 tablespoons cooking sherry | 2 spring onions, sliced |
| 1 tablespoon granulated sweetener | 1 tablespoon toasted sesame seeds |
| 1 tablespoon ground cumin | Hot sauce, for serving |
| 1 teaspoon minced garlic | Lime wedges, for serving |
| Sea salt and freshly ground black pepper, to taste | Flaky sea salt (optional) |

In a small bowl, whisk together the soy sauce, avocado oil, cooking sherry, sweetener, cumin, garlic, and salt and pepper to taste.

Place the steak in a shallow dish. Pour the marinade over the beef. Cover the dish with plastic wrap and let it marinate in the refrigerator for at least 2 hours or overnight.

Remove the flank steak from the dish and discard the marinade.

Set the air fryer to 204ºC. Place the steak in the air fryer basket and air fry for 4 to 6 minutes. Flip the steak and cook for 4 minutes more, until an instant-read thermometer reads 49ºC at the thickest part (or cook it to your desired doneness). Allow the steak to rest for 10 minutes, then slice it thinly against the grain.

Stack 2 lettuce leaves on top of each other and add some sliced meat. Top with spring onions and sesame seeds. Drizzle with hot sauce and lime juice, and finish with a little flaky salt (if using). Repeat with the remaining lettuce leaves and fillings.

## Sichuan Cumin Lamb

### Prep time: 30 minutes | Cook time: 10 minutes | Serves 4

| | |
|---|---|
| Lamb: | 1 tablespoon minced garlic |
| 2 tablespoons cumin seeds | 2 fresh red chiles, chopped |
| 1 teaspoon Sichuan peppercorns, or ½ teaspoon cayenne pepper | 1 teaspoon coarse or flaky salt |
| 450 g lamb (preferably shoulder), cut into ½ by 2-inch pieces | ¼ teaspoon sugar |
| | For Serving: |
| 2 tablespoons vegetable oil | 2 spring onionspring onions, chopped |
| 1 tablespoon light soy sauce | Large handful of chopped fresh coriander |

For the lamb: In a dry skillet, toast the cumin seeds and Sichuan peppercorns (if using) over medium heat, stirring frequently, until fragrant, 1 to 2 minutes. Remove from the heat and let cool. Use a mortar and pestle to coarsely grind the toasted spices.

Use a fork to pierce the lamb pieces to allow the marinade to penetrate better. In a large bowl or resealable plastic bag, combine the toasted spices, vegetable oil, soy sauce, garlic, chiles, salt, and sugar. Add the lamb to the bag. Seal and massage to coat. Marinate at room temperature for 30 minutes.

Place the lamb in a single layer in the air fryer basket. Set the air fryer to 176ºC for 10 minutes. Use a meat thermometer to ensure the lamb has reached an internal temperature of 64ºC (medium-rare). Transfer the lamb to a serving bowl. Stir in the spring onionspring onions and coriander and serve.

## Reuben Beef Rolls with Thousand Island Sauce

### Prep time: 15 minutes | Cook time: 10 minutes per batch | Makes 10 rolls

| | |
|---|---|
| 230 g cooked salt beef, chopped | Thousand Island Sauce: |
| 120 ml drained and chopped sauerkraut | 60 ml chopped dill pickles |
| 1 (230 g) package cream cheese, softened | 60 ml tomato ketchup |
| | 180 ml mayonnaise |
| 120 ml shredded Swiss cheese | Fresh thyme leaves, for garnish |
| 20 slices prosciutto | 2 tablespoons sugar |
| Cooking spray | ⅛ teaspoon fine sea salt |
| | Ground black pepper, to taste |

Preheat the air fryer to 204ºC and spritz with cooking spray.

Combine the beef, sauerkraut, cream cheese, and Swiss cheese in a large bowl. Stir to mix well.

Unroll a slice of prosciutto on a clean work surface, then top with another slice of prosciutto crosswise. Scoop up 4 tablespoons of the beef mixture in the center.

Fold the top slice sides over the filling as the ends of the roll, then roll up the long sides of the bottom prosciutto and make it into a roll shape. Overlap the sides by about 1 inch. Repeat with remaining filling and prosciutto.

Arrange the rolls in the preheated air fryer, seam side down, and spritz with cooking spray.

Air fry for 10 minutes or until golden and crispy. Flip the rolls halfway through. Work in batches to avoid overcrowding.

Meanwhile, combine the ingredients for the sauce in a small bowl. Stir to mix well.

Serve the rolls with the dipping sauce.

## Pork Kebab with Yogurt Sauce

### Prep time: 25 minutes | Cook time: 12 minutes | Serves 4

| | |
|---|---|
| 2 teaspoons olive oil | ½ teaspoon celery salt |
| 230 g pork mince | Yogurt Sauce: |
| 230 g beef mince | 2 tablespoons olive oil |
| 1 egg, whisked | 2 tablespoons fresh lemon juice |
| Sea salt and ground black pepper, to taste | Sea salt, to taste |
| 1 teaspoon paprika | ¼ teaspoon red pepper flakes, crushed |
| 2 garlic cloves, minced | 120 ml full-fat yogurt |
| 1 teaspoon dried marjoram | 1 teaspoon dried dill |
| 1 teaspoon mustard seeds | |

Spritz the sides and bottom of the air fryer basket with 2 teaspoons of olive oil.

In a mixing dish, thoroughly combine the pork, beef, egg, salt, black pepper, paprika, garlic, marjoram, mustard seeds, and celery salt.

Form the mixture into kebabs and transfer them to the greased basket. Cook at 185ºC for 11 to 12 minutes, turning them over once or twice. In the meantime, mix all the sauce ingredients and place in the refrigerator until ready to serve. Serve the pork kebabs with the yogurt sauce on the side. Enjoy!

# Baby Back Ribs

**Prep time: 5 minutes | Cook time: 25 minutes | Serves 4**

900 g baby back ribs
2 teaspoons chili powder
1 teaspoon paprika
½ teaspoon onion granules
½ teaspoon garlic powder

¼ teaspoon ground cayenne pepper
120 ml low-carb, sugar-free barbecue sauce

Rub ribs with all ingredients except barbecue sauce. Place into the air fryer basket.

Adjust the temperature to 204ºC and roast for 25 minutes.

When done, ribs will be dark and charred with an internal temperature of at least 85ºC. Brush ribs with barbecue sauce and serve warm.

# Herbed Lamb Steaks

**Prep time: 30 minutes | Cook time: 15 minutes | Serves 4**

½ medium onion
2 tablespoons minced garlic
2 teaspoons ground ginger
1 teaspoon ground cinnamon
1 teaspoon onion granules

1 teaspoon cayenne pepper
1 teaspoon salt
4 (170 g) boneless lamb sirloin steaks
Oil, for spraying

In a blender, combine the onion, garlic, ginger, cinnamon, onion granules, cayenne pepper, and salt and pulse until the onion is minced.

Place the lamb steaks in a large bowl or zip-top plastic bag and sprinkle the onion mixture over the top. Turn the steaks until they are evenly coated. Cover with plastic wrap or seal the bag and refrigerate for 30 minutes.

Preheat the air fryer to 164ºC. Line the air fryer basket with parchment and spray lightly with oil.

Place the lamb steaks in a single layer in the prepared basket, making sure they don't overlap. You may need to work in batches, depending on the size of your air fryer.

Cook for 8 minutes, flip, and cook for another 7 minutes, or until the internal temperature reaches 68ºC.

# Indian Mint and Chile Kebabs

**Prep time: 30 minutes | Cook time: 15 minutes | Serves 4**

450 g lamb mince
120 ml finely minced onion
60 ml chopped fresh mint
60 ml chopped fresh coriander
1 tablespoon minced garlic

½ teaspoon ground turmeric
½ teaspoon cayenne pepper
¼ teaspoon ground cardamom
¼ teaspoon ground cinnamon
1 teaspoon coarse or flaky salt

In the bowl of a stand mixer fitted with the paddle attachment, combine the lamb, onion, mint, coriander, garlic, turmeric, cayenne, cardamom, cinnamon, and salt.

Mix on low speed until you have a sticky mess of spiced meat. If you have time, let the mixture stand at room temperature for 30 minutes (or cover and refrigerate for up to a day or two, until you're

ready to make the kebabs).

Divide the meat into eight equal portions. Form each into a long sausage shape. Place the kebabs in a single layer in the air fryer basket.

Set the air fryer to 176ºC for 10 minutes. Increase the air fryer temperature to 204ºC and cook for 3 to 4 minutes more to brown the kebabs.

Use a meat thermometer to ensure the kebabs have reached an internal temperature of 72ºC (medium).

# Pork Loin Roast

**Prep time: 30 minutes | Cook time: 55 minutes | Serves 6**

680 g boneless pork loin joint, washed
1 teaspoon mustard seeds
1 teaspoon garlic powder
1 teaspoon porcini powder
1 teaspoon onion granules

¾ teaspoon sea salt flakes
1 teaspoon red pepper flakes, crushed
2 dried sprigs thyme, crushed
2 tablespoons lime juice

Firstly, score the meat using a small knife; make sure to not cut too deep.

In a small-sized mixing dish, combine all seasonings in the order listed above; mix to combine well.

Massage the spice mix into the pork meat to evenly distribute. Drizzle with lemon juice.

Set the air fryer to 182ºC. Place the pork in the air fryer basket; roast for 25 to 30 minutes. Pause the machine, check for doneness and cook for 25 minutes more.

# Italian Sausages with Peppers and Onions

**Prep time: 5 minutes | Cook time: 28 minutes | Serves 3**

1 medium onion, thinly sliced
1 yellow or orange pepper, thinly sliced
1 red pepper, thinly sliced
60 ml avocado oil or melted

coconut oil
1 teaspoon fine sea salt
6 Italian-seasoned sausages
Dijon mustard, for serving (optional)

Preheat the air fryer to 204ºC.

Place the onion and peppers in a large bowl. Drizzle with the oil and toss well to coat the veggies. Season with the salt.

Place the onion and peppers in a pie pan and cook in the air fryer for 8 minutes, stirring halfway through. Remove from the air fryer and set aside.

Spray the air fryer basket with avocado oil. Place the sausages in the air fryer basket and air fry for 20 minutes, or until crispy and golden brown. During the last minute or two of cooking, add the onion and peppers to the basket with the sausages to warm them through.

Place the onion and peppers on a serving platter and arrange the sausages on top. Serve Dijon mustard on the side, if desired.

Store leftovers in an airtight container in the fridge for up to 7 days or in the freezer for up to a month. Reheat in a preheated 200ºC air fryer for 3 minutes, or until heated through.

## Sweet and Spicy Country-Style Ribs

### Prep time: 10 minutes | Cook time: 25 minutes | Serves 4

2 tablespoons brown sugar
2 tablespoons smoked paprika
1 teaspoon garlic powder
1 teaspoon onion granules
1 teaspoon mustard powder
1 teaspoon ground cumin
1 teaspoon coarse or flaky salt
1 teaspoon black pepper
¼ to ½ teaspoon cayenne pepper
680 g boneless pork steaks
235 ml barbecue sauce

In a small bowl, stir together the brown sugar, paprika, garlic powder, onion granules, mustard powder, cumin, salt, black pepper, and cayenne. Mix until well combined.

Pat the ribs dry with a paper towel. Generously sprinkle the rub evenly over both sides of the ribs and rub in with your fingers.

Place the ribs in the air fryer basket. Set the air fryer to 176ºC for 15 minutes. Turn the ribs and brush with 120 ml of the barbecue sauce. Cook for an additional 10 minutes.

Use a meat thermometer to ensure the pork has reached an internal temperature of 64ºC.

Serve with remaining barbecue sauce.

## Vietnamese Grilled Pork

### Prep time: 30 minutes | Cook time: 20 minutes | Serves 6

60 ml minced brown onion
2 tablespoons sugar
2 tablespoons vegetable oil
1 tablespoon minced garlic
1 tablespoon fish sauce
1 tablespoon minced fresh lemongrass
2 teaspoons dark soy sauce
½ teaspoon black pepper
680 g boneless pork shoulder, cut into ½-inch-thick slices
60 ml chopped salted roasted peanuts
2 tablespoons chopped fresh coriander or parsley

In a large bowl, combine the onion, sugar, vegetable oil, garlic, fish sauce, lemongrass, soy sauce, and pepper. Add the pork and toss to coat.

Marinate at room temperature for 30 minutes, or cover and refrigerate for up to 24 hours.

Arrange the pork slices in the air fryer basket; discard the marinade. Set the air fryer to 204ºC for 20 minutes, turning the pork halfway through the cooking time.

Transfer the pork to a serving platter. Sprinkle with the peanuts and coriander and serve.

## Bacon, Cheese and Pear Stuffed Pork

### Prep time: 10 minutes | Cook time: 24 minutes | Serves 3

4 slices bacon, chopped
1 tablespoon butter
120 ml finely diced onion
80 ml chicken stock
355 ml seasoned stuffing mix
1 egg, beaten
½ teaspoon dried thyme
½ teaspoon salt
⅛ teaspoon black pepper
1 pear, finely diced
80 ml crumbled blue cheese
3 boneless pork chops (2-inch thick)
Olive oil
Salt and freshly ground black pepper, to taste

Preheat the air fryer to 204ºC.

Place the bacon into the air fryer basket and air fry for 6 minutes, stirring halfway through the cooking time. Remove the bacon and set it aside on a paper towel. Pour out the grease from the bottom of the air fryer.

Make the stuffing:

Melt the butter in a medium saucepan over medium heat on the stovetop. Add the onion and sauté for a few minutes, until it starts to soften. Add the chicken stock and simmer for 1 minute.

Remove the pan from the heat and add the stuffing mix. Stir until the stock has been absorbed. Add the egg, dried thyme, salt and freshly ground black pepper, and stir until combined. Fold in the diced pear and crumbled blue cheese.

Place the pork chops on a cutting board. Using the palm of your hand to hold the chop flat and steady, slice into the side of the pork chop to make a pocket in the center of the chop.

Leave about an inch of chop uncut and make sure you don't cut all the way through the pork chop. Brush both sides of the pork chops with olive oil and season with salt and freshly ground black pepper. Stuff each pork chop with a third of the stuffing, packing the stuffing tightly inside the pocket.

Preheat the air fryer to 182ºC.

Spray or brush the sides of the air fryer basket with oil. Place the pork chops in the air fryer basket with the open stuffed edge of the pork chop facing the outside edges of the basket.

Air fry the pork chops for 18 minutes, turning the pork chops over halfway through the cooking time. When the chops are done, let them rest for 5 minutes and then transfer to a serving platter.

## Fajita Meatball Lettuce Wraps

### Prep time: 10 minutes | Cook time: 10 minutes | Serves 4

450 g beef mince (85% lean)
120 ml salsa, plus more for serving if desired
60 ml chopped onions
60 ml diced green or red peppers
1 large egg, beaten
1 teaspoon fine sea salt
½ teaspoon chili powder
½ teaspoon ground cumin
1 clove garlic, minced
For Serving (Optional):
8 leaves butterhead lettuce
Pico de gallo or salsa
Lime slices

Spray the air fryer basket with avocado oil. Preheat the air fryer to 176ºC.

In a large bowl, mix together all the ingredients until well combined.

Shape the meat mixture into eight 1-inch balls. Place the meatballs in the air fryer basket, leaving a little space between them. Air fry for 10 minutes, or until cooked through and no longer pink inside and the internal temperature reaches 64ºC.

Serve each meatball on a lettuce leaf, topped with pico de gallo or salsa, if desired. Serve with lime slices if desired.

Store leftovers in an airtight container in the fridge for 3 days or in the freezer for up to a month. Reheat in a preheated 176ºC air fryer for 4 minutes, or until heated through.

# Peppercorn-Crusted Beef Fillet

**Prep time: 10 minutes | Cook time: 25 minutes | Serves 6**

2 tablespoons salted butter, melted
2 teaspoons minced roasted garlic
3 tablespoons ground 4-peppercorn blend
1 (900 g) beef fillet, trimmed of visible fat

In a small bowl, mix the butter and roasted garlic. Brush it over the beef fillet.
Place the ground peppercorns onto a plate and roll the fillet through them, creating a crust. Place fillet into the air fryer basket.
Adjust the temperature to 204ºC and roast for 25 minutes.
Turn the fillet halfway through the cooking time.
Allow meat to rest 10 minutes before slicing.

# Italian Lamb Chops with Avocado Mayo

**Prep time: 5 minutes | Cook time: 12 minutes | Serves 2**

2 lamp chops
2 teaspoons Italian herbs
2 avocados
120 ml mayonnaise
1 tablespoon lemon juice

Season the lamb chops with the Italian herbs, then set aside for 5 minutes.
Preheat the air fryer to 204ºC and place the rack inside.
Put the chops on the rack and air fry for 12 minutes.
In the meantime, halve the avocados and open to remove the pits. Spoon the flesh into a blender.
Add the mayonnaise and lemon juice and pulse until a smooth consistency is achieved.
Take care when removing the chops from the air fryer, then plate up and serve with the avocado mayo.

# Easy Lamb Chops with Asparagus

**Prep time: 10 minutes | Cook time: 15 minutes | Serves 4**

4 asparagus spears, trimmed
2 tablespoons olive oil, divided
450 g lamb chops
1 garlic clove, minced
2 teaspoons chopped fresh thyme, for serving
Salt and ground black pepper, to taste

Preheat the air fryer to 204ºC. Spritz the air fryer basket with cooking spray.
On a large plate, brush the asparagus with 1 tablespoon olive oil, then sprinkle with salt. Set aside.
On a separate plate, brush the lamb chops with remaining olive oil and sprinkle with salt and ground black pepper.
Arrange the lamb chops in the preheated air fryer. Air fry for 10 minutes.
Flip the lamb chops and add the asparagus and garlic. Air fry for 5 more minutes or until the lamb is well browned and the asparagus is tender.
Serve them on a plate with thyme on top.

# Barbecue Ribs

**Prep time: 5 minutes | Cook time: 30 minutes | Serves 4**

1 (900 g) rack baby back ribs
1 teaspoon onion granules
1 teaspoon garlic powder
1 teaspoon light brown sugar
1 teaspoon dried oregano
Salt and freshly ground black pepper, to taste
Cooking oil spray
120 ml barbecue sauce

Use a sharp knife to remove the thin membrane from the back of the ribs. Cut the rack in half, or as needed, so the ribs fit in the air fryer basket. The best way to do this is to cut the ribs into 4- or 5-rib sections.
In a small bowl, stir together the onion granules, garlic powder, brown sugar, and oregano and season with salt and pepper. Rub the spice seasoning onto the front and back of the ribs.
Cover the ribs with plastic wrap or foil and let sit at room temperature for 30 minutes.
Insert the crisper plate into the basket and the basket into the unit. Preheat the unit by selecting AIR ROAST, setting the temperature to 182ºC, and setting the time to 3 minutes. Select START/STOP to begin.
Once the unit is preheated, spray the crisper plate with cooking oil. Place the ribs into the basket. It is okay to stack them.
Select AIR ROAST, set the temperature to 182ºC, and set the time to 30 minutes. Select START/STOP to begin.
After 15 minutes, flip the ribs. Resume cooking for 15 minutes, or until a food thermometer registers 88ºC.
When the cooking is complete, transfer the ribs to a serving dish. Drizzle the ribs with the barbecue sauce and serve.

# Pork Loin with Aloha Salsa

**Prep time: 20 minutes | Cook time: 7 to 9 minutes | Serves 4**

Aloha Salsa:
235 ml fresh pineapple, chopped in small pieces
60 ml red onion, finely chopped
60 ml green or red pepper, chopped
½ teaspoon ground cinnamon
1 teaspoon reduced-salt soy sauce
⅛ teaspoon crushed red pepper
⅛ teaspoon ground black pepper
2 eggs
2 tablespoons milk
60 ml flour
60 ml panko bread crumbs
4 teaspoons sesame seeds
450 g boneless, thin pork loin or tenderloin (⅜- to ½-inch thick)
Pepper and salt
60 ml corn flour
Oil for misting or cooking spray

In a medium bowl, stir together all ingredients for salsa. Cover and refrigerate while cooking pork.
Preheat the air fryer to 200ºC.
Beat together eggs and milk in shallow dish.
In another shallow dish, mix together the flour, panko, and sesame seeds.
Sprinkle pork with pepper and salt to taste.
Dip pork in corn flour, egg mixture, and then panko coating. Spray both sides with oil or cooking spray.
Cook pork for 3 minutes. Turn pork over, spraying both sides, and continue cooking for 4 to 6 minutes or until well done.
Serve fried cutlets with salsa on the side.

## Teriyaki Rump Steak with Broccoli and Capsicum

**Prep time: 5 minutes | Cook time: 13 minutes | Serves 4**

230 g rump steak
80 ml teriyaki marinade
1½ teaspoons sesame oil
½ head broccoli, cut into florets

2 red peppers, sliced
Fine sea salt and ground black pepper, to taste
Cooking spray

Toss the rump steak in a large bowl with teriyaki marinade. Wrap the bowl in plastic and refrigerate to marinate for at least an hour.
Preheat the air fryer to 204ºC and spritz with cooking spray.
Discard the marinade and transfer the steak in the preheated air fryer. Spritz with cooking spray.
Air fry for 13 minutes or until well browned. Flip the steak halfway through.
Meanwhile, heat the sesame oil in a nonstick skillet over medium heat. Add the broccoli and red pepper. Sprinkle with salt and ground black pepper. Sauté for 5 minutes or until the broccoli is tender.
Transfer the air fried rump steak on a plate and top with the sautéed broccoli and pepper. Serve hot.

## Mexican-Style Shredded Beef

**Prep time: 5 minutes | Cook time: 35 minutes | Serves 6**

1 (900 g) beef braising steak, cut into 2-inch cubes
1 teaspoon salt

½ teaspoon ground black pepper
120 ml no-sugar-added chipotle sauce

In a large bowl, sprinkle beef cubes with salt and pepper and toss to coat. Place beef into ungreased air fryer basket.
Adjust the temperature to 204ºC and air fry for 30 minutes, shaking the basket halfway through cooking. Beef will be done when internal temperature is at least 72ºC.
Place cooked beef into a large bowl and shred with two forks. Pour in chipotle sauce and toss to coat.
Return beef to air fryer basket for an additional 5 minutes at 204ºC to crisp with sauce. Serve warm.

## Tomato and Bacon Zoodles

**Prep time: 10 minutes | Cook time: 15 to 22 minutes | Serves 2**

230 g sliced bacon
120 ml baby plum tomatoes
1 large courgette, spiralized
120 ml ricotta cheese
60 ml double/whipping cream

80 ml finely grated Parmesan cheese, plus more for serving
Sea salt and freshly ground black pepper, to taste

Set the air fryer to 204ºC. Arrange the bacon strips in a single layer in the air fryer basket—some overlapping is okay because the bacon will shrink, but cook in batches if needed. Air fry for 8 minutes. Flip the bacon strips and air fry for 2 to 5 minutes more, until the bacon is crisp. Remove the bacon from the air fryer.
Put the tomatoes in the air fryer basket and air fry for 3 to 5

minutes, until they are just starting to burst. Remove the tomatoes from the air fryer.
Put the courgette noodles in the air fryer and air fry for 2 to 4 minutes, to the desired doneness.
Meanwhile, combine the ricotta, cream, and Parmesan in a saucepan over medium-low heat. Cook, stirring often, until warm and combined.
Crumble the bacon. Place the courgette, bacon, and tomatoes in a bowl. Toss with the ricotta sauce. Season with salt and pepper, and sprinkle with additional Parmesan.

## 900 g beef bavette or skirt steak

**6 slices low-moisture Mozarella or other melting cheese**

85 g roasted red peppers
180 ml baby spinach

1 teaspoon sea salt
1 teaspoon black pepper

Preheat the air fryer to 204ºC.
Spoon equal amounts of the pesto onto each steak and spread it across evenly.
Put the cheese, roasted red peppers and spinach on top of the meat, about three-quarters of the way down.
Roll the steak up, holding it in place with toothpicks. Sprinkle with the sea salt and pepper.
Put inside the air fryer and air fry for 14 minutes, turning halfway through the cooking time.
Allow the beef to rest for 10 minutes before slicing up and serving.

## Steaks with Walnut-Blue Cheese Butter

**Prep time: 30 minutes | Cook time: 10 minutes | Serves 6**

120 ml unsalted butter, at room temperature
120 ml crumbled blue cheese
2 tablespoons finely chopped walnuts
1 tablespoon minced fresh rosemary

1 teaspoon minced garlic
¼ teaspoon cayenne pepper
Sea salt and freshly ground black pepper, to taste
680 g sirloin steaks, at room temperature

In a medium bowl, combine the butter, blue cheese, walnuts, rosemary, garlic, and cayenne pepper and salt and black pepper to taste. Use clean hands to ensure that everything is well combined.
Place the mixture on a sheet of parchment paper and form it into a log. Wrap it tightly in plastic wrap. Refrigerate for at least 2 hours or freeze for 30 minutes.
Season the steaks generously with salt and pepper.
Place the air fryer basket or grill pan in the air fryer. Set the air fryer to 204ºC and let it preheat for 5 minutes.
Place the steaks in the basket in a single layer and air fry for 5 minutes. Flip the steaks, and cook for 5 minutes more, until an instant-read thermometer reads 49ºC for medium-rare (or as desired).
Transfer the steaks to a plate. Cut the butter into pieces and place the desired amount on top of the steaks. Tent a piece of aluminum foil over the steaks and allow to sit for 10 minutes before serving.
Store any remaining butter in a sealed container in the refrigerator for up to 2 weeks.

## Filipino Crispy Pork Belly

**Prep time: 20 minutes | Cook time: 30 minutes | Serves 4**

450 g pork belly
700 ml water
6 garlic cloves
2 tablespoons soy sauce
1 teaspoon coarse or flaky salt
1 teaspoon black pepper
2 bay leaves

Cut the pork belly into three thick chunks so it will cook more evenly.
Place the pork, water, garlic, soy sauce, salt, pepper, and bay leaves in the inner pot of an Instant Pot or other electric pressure cooker. Seal and cook at high pressure for 15 minutes.
Let the pressure release naturally for 10 minutes, then manually release the remaining pressure. (If you do not have a pressure cooker, place all the ingredients in a large saucepan. Cover and cook over low heat until a knife can be easily inserted into the skin side of pork belly, about 1 hour.)
Using tongs, very carefully transfer the meat to a wire rack over a rimmed baking sheet to drain and dry for 10 minutes.
Cut each chunk of pork belly into two long slices. Arrange the slices in the air fryer basket. Set the air fryer to 204ºC for 15 minutes, or until the fat has crisped.
Serve immediately.

## Herbed Beef

**Prep time: 5 minutes | Cook time: 22 minutes | Serves 6**

1 teaspoon dried dill
1 teaspoon dried thyme
1 teaspoon garlic powder
900 g beef steak
3 tablespoons butter

Preheat the air fryer to 182ºC.
Combine the dill, thyme, and garlic powder in a small bowl, and massage into the steak.
Air fry the steak in the air fryer for 20 minutes, then remove, shred, and return to the air fryer.
Add the butter and air fry the shredded steak for a further 2 minutes at 185ºC. Make sure the beef is coated in the butter before serving.
Beef and Spinach Rolls
Prep time: 10 minutes | Cook time: 14 minutes | Serves 2
3 teaspoons pesto

## Spice-Rubbed Pork Loin

**Prep time: 5 minutes | Cook time: 20 minutes | Serves 6**

1 teaspoon paprika
½ teaspoon ground cumin
½ teaspoon chili powder
½ teaspoon garlic powder
2 tablespoons coconut oil
1 (680 g) boneless pork loin
½ teaspoon salt
¼ teaspoon ground black pepper

In a small bowl, mix paprika, cumin, chili powder, and garlic powder.
Drizzle coconut oil over pork. Sprinkle pork loin with salt and pepper, then rub spice mixture evenly on all sides.

Place pork loin into ungreased air fryer basket. Adjust the temperature to 204ºC and air fry for 20 minutes, turning pork halfway through cooking. Pork loin will be browned and have an internal temperature of at least 64ºC when done. Serve warm.

## Bacon and Cheese Stuffed Pork Chops

**Prep time: 10 minutes | Cook time: 12 minutes | Serves 4**

15 g plain pork scratchings, finely crushed
120 ml shredded sharp Cheddar cheese
4 slices cooked bacon, crumbled
4 (110 g) boneless pork chops
½ teaspoon salt
¼ teaspoon ground black pepper

In a small bowl, mix pork scratchings, Cheddar, and bacon.
Make a 3-inch slit in the side of each pork chop and stuff with ¼ pork rind mixture. Sprinkle each side of pork chops with salt and pepper.
Place pork chops into ungreased air fryer basket, stuffed side up. Adjust the temperature to 204ºC and air fry for 12 minutes. Pork chops will be browned and have an internal temperature of at least 64ºC when done. Serve warm.

## Nigerian Peanut-Crusted Bavette Steak

**Prep time: 30 minutes | Cook time: 8 minutes | Serves 4**

Suya Spice Mix:
60 ml dry-roasted peanuts
1 teaspoon cumin seeds
1 teaspoon garlic powder
1 teaspoon smoked paprika
½ teaspoon ground ginger
1 teaspoon coarse or flaky salt
½ teaspoon cayenne pepper
Steak:
450 g bavette or skirt steak
2 tablespoons vegetable oil

For the spice mix:
In a clean coffee grinder or spice mill, combine the peanuts and cumin seeds. Process until you get a coarse powder. (Do not overprocess or you will wind up with peanut butter! Alternatively, you can grind the cumin with 80 ml ready-made peanut powder instead of the peanuts.)
Pour the peanut mixture into a small bowl, add the garlic powder, paprika, ginger, salt, and cayenne, and stir to combine. This recipe makes about 120 ml suya spice mix. Store leftovers in an airtight container in a cool, dry place for up to 1 month.
For the steak:
Cut the steak into ½-inch-thick slices, cutting against the grain and at a slight angle. Place the beef strips in a resealable plastic bag and add the oil and 2½ to 3 tablespoons of the spice mixture.
Seal the bag and massage to coat all of the meat with the oil and spice mixture. Marinate at room temperature for 30 minutes or in the refrigerator for up to 24 hours.
Place the beef strips in the air fryer basket. Set the air fryer to 204ºC for 8 minutes, turning the strips halfway through the cooking time.
Transfer the meat to a serving platter. Sprinkle with additional spice mix, if desired.

# Rosemary Roast Beef

**Prep time: 30 minutes | Cook time: 30 to 35 minutes | Serves 8**

1 (900 g) beef roasting joint, tied with kitchen string
Sea salt and freshly ground black pepper, to taste

2 teaspoons minced garlic
2 tablespoons finely chopped fresh rosemary
60 ml avocado oil

Season the roast generously with salt and pepper.

In a small bowl, whisk together the garlic, rosemary, and avocado oil. Rub this all over the roast. Cover loosely with aluminum foil or plastic wrap and refrigerate for at least 12 hours or up to 2 days.

Remove the roast from the refrigerator and allow to sit at room temperature for about 1 hour.

Set the air fryer to 164ºC. Place the roast in the air fryer basket and roast for 15 minutes. Flip the roast and cook for 15 to 20 minutes more, until the meat is browned and an instant-read thermometer reads 49ºC at the thickest part (for medium-rare).

Transfer the meat to a cutting board, and let it rest for 15 minutes before thinly slicing and serving.

# Spicy Lamb Sirloin Chops

**Prep time: 30 minutes | Cook time: 15 minutes | Serves 4**

½ brown onion, coarsely chopped
4 coin-size slices peeled fresh ginger
5 garlic cloves
1 teaspoon garam masala

1 teaspoon ground fennel
1 teaspoon ground cinnamon
1 teaspoon ground turmeric
½ to 1 teaspoon cayenne pepper
½ teaspoon ground cardamom
1 teaspoon coarse or flaky salt
450 g lamb sirloin chops

In a blender, combine the onion, ginger, garlic, garam masala, fennel, cinnamon, turmeric, cayenne, cardamom, and salt. Pulse until the onion is finely minced and the mixture forms a thick paste, 3 to 4 minutes.

Place the lamb chops in a large bowl. Slash the meat and fat with a sharp knife several times to allow the marinade to penetrate better. Add the spice paste to the bowl and toss the lamb to coat. Marinate at room temperature for 30 minutes or cover and refrigerate for up to 24 hours.

Place the lamb chops in a single layer in the air fryer basket. Set the air fryer to 164ºC for 15 minutes, turning the chops halfway through the cooking time. Use a meat thermometer to ensure the lamb has reached an internal temperature of 64ºC (medium-rare).

# Honey-Baked Pork Loin

**Prep time: 30 minutes | Cook time: 22 to 25 minutes | Serves 6**

60 ml honey
60 ml freshly squeezed lemon juice
2 tablespoons soy sauce

1 teaspoon garlic powder
1 (900 g) pork loin
2 tablespoons vegetable oil

In a medium bowl, whisk together the honey, lemon juice, soy sauce, and garlic powder. Reserve half of the mixture for basting during cooking.

Cut 5 slits in the pork loin and transfer it to a resealable bag. Add the remaining honey mixture. Seal the bag and refrigerate to marinate for at least 2 hours.

Preheat the air fryer to 204ºC. Line the air fryer basket with parchment paper.

Remove the pork from the marinade, and place it on the parchment. Spritz with oil, then baste with the reserved marinade.

Cook for 15 minutes. Flip the pork, baste with more marinade and spritz with oil again. Cook for 7 to 10 minutes more until the internal temperature reaches 64ºC. Let rest for 5 minutes before serving.

# Kheema Meatloaf

**Prep time: 10 minutes | Cook time: 15 minutes | Serves 4**

450 g 85% lean beef mince
2 large eggs, lightly beaten
235 ml diced brown onion
60 ml chopped fresh coriander
1 tablespoon minced fresh ginger
1 tablespoon minced garlic

2 teaspoons garam masala
1 teaspoon coarse or flaky salt
1 teaspoon ground turmeric
1 teaspoon cayenne pepper
½ teaspoon ground cinnamon
⅛ teaspoon ground cardamom

In a large bowl, gently mix the beef mince, eggs, onion, coriander, ginger, garlic, garam masala, salt, turmeric, cayenne, cinnamon, and cardamom until thoroughly combined.

Place the seasoned meat in a baking pan. Place the pan in the air fryer basket. Set the air fryer to 176ºC for 15 minutes. Use a meat thermometer to ensure the meat loaf has reached an internal temperature of 72ºC (medium).

Drain the fat and liquid from the pan and let stand for 5 minutes before slicing.

Slice and serve hot.

# Cheese Wine Pork Loin

**Prep time: 30 minutes | Cook time: 15 minutes | Serves 2**

235 ml water
235 ml red wine
1 tablespoon sea salt
2 pork loin steaks
60 ml ground almonds
60 ml flaxseed meal
½ teaspoon baking powder
1 teaspoon onion granules

½ teaspoon porcini powder
Sea salt and ground black pepper, to taste
1 egg
60 ml yoghurt
1 teaspoon wholegrain or English mustard
80 ml Parmesan cheese, grated

In a large ceramic dish, combine the water, wine and salt. Add the pork and put for 1 hour in the refrigerator.

In a shallow bowl, mix the ground almonds, flaxseed meal, baking powder, onion granules, porcini powder, salt, and ground pepper. In another bowl, whisk the eggs with yoghurt and mustard.

In a third bowl, place the grated Parmesan cheese.

Dip the pork in the seasoned flour mixture and toss evenly; then, in the egg mixture. Finally, roll them over the grated Parmesan cheese.

Spritz the bottom of the air fryer basket with cooking oil. Add the breaded pork and cook at 202ºC and for 10 minutes.

Flip and cook for 5 minutes more on the other side. Serve warm.

## Bacon-Wrapped Pork Tenderloin

**Prep time: 30 minutes | Cook time: 22 to 25 minutes | Serves 6**

120 ml minced onion
120 ml apple cider, or apple juice
60 ml honey
1 tablespoon minced garlic
¼ teaspoon salt
¼ teaspoon freshly ground black pepper
900 g pork tenderloin
1 to 2 tablespoons oil
8 uncooked bacon slices

In a medium bowl, stir together the onion, cider, honey, garlic, salt, and pepper. Transfer to a large resealable bag or airtight container and add the pork. Seal the bag. Refrigerate to marinate for at least 2 hours.
Preheat the air fryer to 204°C. Line the air fryer basket with parchment paper.
Remove the pork from the marinade and place it on the parchment. Spritz with oil.
Cook for 15 minutes.
Wrap the bacon slices around the pork and secure them with toothpicks. Turn the pork roast and spritz with oil. Cook for 7 to 10 minutes more until the internal temperature reaches 64°C, depending on how well-done you like pork loin.
It will continue cooking after it's removed from the fryer, so let it sit for 5 minutes before serving.

## Zesty London Broil

**Prep time: 30 minutes | Cook time: 20 to 28 minutes | Serves 4 to 6**

160 ml ketchup
60 ml honey
60 ml olive oil
2 tablespoons apple cider vinegar
2 tablespoons Worcestershire sauce
2 tablespoons minced onion
½ teaspoon paprika
1 teaspoon salt
1 teaspoon freshly ground black pepper
900 g bavette or skirt steak (about 1-inch thick)

Combine the ketchup, honey, olive oil, apple cider vinegar, Worcestershire sauce, minced onion, paprika, salt and pepper in a small bowl and whisk together.
Generously pierce both sides of the meat with a fork or meat tenderizer and place it in a shallow dish. Pour the marinade mixture over the steak, making sure all sides of the meat get coated with the marinade. Cover and refrigerate overnight.
Preheat the air fryer to 204°C.
Transfer the steak to the air fryer basket and air fry for 20 to 28 minutes, depending on how rare or well done you like your steak. Flip the steak over halfway through the cooking time.
Remove the steak from the air fryer and let it rest for five minutes on a cutting board. To serve, thinly slice the meat against the grain and transfer to a serving platter.

## Roast Beef with Horseradish Cream

**Prep time: 5 minutes | Cook time: 35 to 45 minutes | Serves 6**

900 g beef roasting joint
1 tablespoon salt
2 teaspoons garlic powder
1 teaspoon freshly ground black pepper
1 teaspoon dried thyme
Horseradish Cream:
80 ml double cream
80 ml sour cream
80 ml grated horseradish
2 teaspoons fresh lemon juice
Salt and freshly ground black pepper, to taste

Preheat the air fryer to 204°C.
Season the beef with the salt, garlic powder, black pepper, and thyme. Place the beef fat-side down in the basket of the air fryer and lightly coat with olive oil.
Pausing halfway through the cooking time to turn the meat, air fry for 35 to 45 minutes, until a thermometer inserted into the thickest part indicates the desired doneness, 52°C (rare) to 64°C (medium).
Let the beef rest for 10 minutes before slicing.
To make the horseradish cream:
In a small bowl, combine the double cream, sour cream, horseradish, and lemon juice. Whisk until thoroughly combined. Season to taste with salt and freshly ground black pepper. Serve alongside the beef.

# Chapter 6 Fish and Seafood

# Chapter 6 Fish and Seafood

## Tilapia with Pecans

**Prep time: 20 minutes | Cook time: 16 minutes | Serves 5**

2 tablespoons ground flaxseeds
1 teaspoon paprika
Sea salt and white pepper, to taste
1 teaspoon garlic paste

2 tablespoons extra-virgin olive oil
65 g pecans, ground
5 tilapia fillets, sliced into halves

Combine the ground flaxseeds, paprika, salt, white pepper, garlic paste, olive oil, and ground pecans in a sealable freezer bag. Add the fish fillets and shake to coat well.
Spritz the air fryer basket with cooking spray. Cook in the preheated air fryer at 204ºC for 10 minutes; turn them over and cook for 6 minutes more. Work in batches.
Serve with lemon wedges, if desired. Enjoy!

## Sesame-Crusted Tuna Steak

**Prep time: 5 minutes | Cook time: 8 minutes | Serves 2**

2 tuna steaks, 170 g each
1 tablespoon coconut oil, melted
½ teaspoon garlic powder

2 teaspoons white sesame seeds
2 teaspoons black sesame seeds

Brush each tuna steak with coconut oil and sprinkle with garlic powder.
In a large bowl, mix sesame seeds and then press each tuna steak into them, covering the steak as completely as possible. Place tuna steaks into the air fryer basket.
Adjust the temperature to 204ºC and air fry for 8 minutes.
Flip the steaks halfway through the cooking time. Steaks will be well-done at 64ºC internal temperature. Serve warm.

## Lemon Pepper Prawns

**Prep time: 15 minutes | Cook time: 8 minutes | Serves 2**

Olive or vegetable oil, for spraying
340 g medium raw prawns, peeled and deveined
3 tablespoons lemon juice

1 tablespoon olive oil
1 teaspoon lemon pepper
¼ teaspoon paprika
¼ teaspoon granulated garlic

Preheat the air fryer to 204ºC. Line the air fryer basket with baking paper and spray lightly with oil.
In a medium bowl, toss together the prawns, lemon juice, olive oil, lemon pepper, paprika, and garlic until evenly coated.
Place the prawns in the prepared basket.
Cook for 6 to 8 minutes, or until pink and firm. Serve immediately.

## Orange-Mustard Glazed Salmon

**Prep time: 10 minutes | Cook time: 10 minutes | Serves 2**

1 tablespoon orange marmalade
¼ teaspoon grated orange zest plus 1 tablespoon juice
2 teaspoons whole-grain mustard

2 (230 g) skin-on salmon fillets, 1½ inches thick
Salt and pepper, to taste
Vegetable oil spray

Preheat the air fryer to 204ºC.
Make foil sling for air fryer basket by folding 1 long sheet of aluminum foil so it is 4 inches wide. Lay sheet of foil widthwise across basket, pressing foil into and up sides of basket.
Fold excess foil as needed so that edges of foil are flush with top of basket. Lightly spray foil and basket with vegetable oil spray.
Combine marmalade, orange zest and juice, and mustard in bowl. Pat salmon dry with paper towels and season with salt and pepper. Brush tops and sides of fillets evenly with glaze.
Arrange fillets skin side down on sling in prepared basket, spaced evenly apart. Air fry salmon until center is still translucent when checked with the tip of a paring knife and registers 52ºC (for medium-rare), 10 to 14 minutes, using sling to rotate fillets halfway through cooking.
Using the sling, carefully remove salmon from air fryer. Slide fish spatula along underside of fillets and transfer to individual serving plates, leaving skin behind. Serve.

## Fried Catfish with Dijon Sauce

**Prep time: 20 minutes | Cook time: 7 minutes | Serves 4**

4 tablespoons butter, melted
2 teaspoons Worcestershire sauce, divided
1 teaspoon lemon pepper
120 g panko bread crumbs

4 catfish fillets, 110g each
Cooking spray
120 ml sour cream
1 tablespoon Dijon mustard

In a shallow bowl, stir together the melted butter, 1 teaspoon of Worcestershire sauce, and the lemon pepper. Place the bread crumbs in another shallow bowl.
One at a time, dip both sides of the fillets in the butter mixture, then the bread crumbs, coating thoroughly.
Preheat the air fryer to 150ºC. Line the air fryer basket with baking paper.
Place the coated fish on the baking paper and spritz with oil.
Bake for 4 minutes. Flip the fish, spritz it with oil, and bake for 3 to 6 minutes more, depending on the thickness of the fillets, until the fish flakes easily with a fork.
In a small bowl, stir together the sour cream, Dijon, and remaining 1 teaspoon of Worcestershire sauce. This sauce can be made 1 day in advance and refrigerated before serving. Serve with the fried fish.

## Prawns with Swiss Chard

**Prep time: 10 minutes | Cook time: 10 minutes | Serves 4**

455 g prawns, peeled and deveined
½ teaspoon smoked paprika
70 g Swiss chard, chopped

2 tablespoons apple cider vinegar
1 tablespoon coconut oil
60 ml heavy cream

Mix prawns with smoked paprika and apple cider vinegar.
Put the prawns in the air fryer and add coconut oil.
Cook the prawns at 176ºC for 10 minutes.
Then mix cooked prawns with remaining ingredients and carefully mix.

## Pecan-Crusted Tilapia

**Prep time: 10minutes | Cook time: 10 minutes | Serves 4**

160 g pecans
45 g panko bread crumbs
70 g plain flour
2 tablespoons Cajun seasoning
2 eggs, beaten with 2

tablespoons water
4 tilapia fillets, 170g each
Vegetable oil, for spraying
Lemon wedges, for serving

Grind the pecans in the food processor until they resemble coarse meal. Combine the ground pecans with the panko on a plate. On a second plate, combine the flour and Cajun seasoning.
Dry the tilapia fillets using paper towels and dredge them in the flour mixture, shaking off any excess. Dip the fillets in the egg mixture and then dredge them in the pecan and panko mixture, pressing the coating onto the fillets.
Place the breaded fillets on a plate or rack.
Preheat the air fryer to 192ºC. Spray both sides of the breaded fillets with oil.
Carefully transfer 2 of the fillets to the air fryer basket and air fry for 9 to 10 minutes, flipping once halfway through, until the flesh is opaque and flaky. Repeat with the remaining fillets.
Serve immediately with lemon wedges.

## Seasoned Tuna Steaks

**Prep time: 5 minutes | Cook time: 9 minutes | Serves 4**

1 teaspoon garlic powder
½ teaspoon salt
¼ teaspoon dried thyme
¼ teaspoon dried oregano

4 tuna steaks
2 tablespoons olive oil
1 lemon, quartered

Preheat the air fryer to 192ºC.
In a small bowl, whisk together the garlic powder, salt, thyme, and oregano.
Coat the tuna steaks with olive oil. Season both sides of each steak with the seasoning blend. Place the steaks in a single layer in the air fryer basket.
Roast for 5 minutes, then flip and roast for an additional 3 to 4 minutes.

## Thai Prawn Skewers with Peanut Dipping Sauce

**Prep time: 15 minutes | Cook time: 6 minutes | Serves 2**

Salt and pepper, to taste
340 g extra-large prawns, peeled and deveined
1 tablespoon vegetable oil
1 teaspoon honey
½ teaspoon grated lime zest plus 1 tablespoon juice, plus lime wedges for serving

6 (6-inch) wooden skewers
3 tablespoons creamy peanut butter
3 tablespoons hot tap water
1 tablespoon chopped fresh coriander
1 teaspoon fish sauce

Preheat the air fryer to 204ºC.
Dissolve 2 tablespoons salt in 1 litre cold water in a large container. Add prawns, cover, and refrigerate for 15 minutes.
Remove prawns from brine and pat dry with paper towels. Whisk oil, honey, lime zest, and ¼ teaspoon pepper together in a large bowl.
Add prawns and toss to coat. Thread prawns onto skewers, leaving about ¼ inch between each prawns (3 or 4 prawns per skewer).
Arrange 3 skewers in air fryer basket, parallel to each other and spaced evenly apart. Arrange remaining 3 skewers on top, perpendicular to the bottom layer.
Air fry until prawns are opaque throughout, 6 to 8 minutes, flipping and rotating skewers halfway through cooking.
Whisk peanut butter, hot tap water, lime juice, coriander, and fish sauce together in a bowl until smooth. Serve skewers with peanut dipping sauce and lime wedges.

## Crustless Prawn Quiche

**Prep time: 15 minutes | Cook time: 20 minutes | Serves 2**

Vegetable oil
4 large eggs
120 ml single cream
110 g raw prawns, chopped
120 g shredded Parmesan or Swiss cheese
235 g chopped spring onions

1 teaspoon sweet smoked paprika
1 teaspoon Herbes de Provence
1 teaspoon black pepper
½ to 1 teaspoon kosher or coarse sea salt

Generously grease a baking pan with vegetable oil. (Be sure to grease the pan well, the proteins in eggs stick something fierce. Alternatively, line the bottom of the pan with baking paper cut to fit and spray the baking paper and sides of the pan generously with vegetable oil spray.)
In a large bowl, beat together the eggs and single cream. Add the prawns, 90 g of the cheese, the scallions, paprika, Herbes de Provence, pepper, and salt. Stir with a fork to thoroughly combine. Pour the egg mixture into the prepared pan.
Place the pan in the air fryer basket. Set the air fryer to 150ºC for 20 minutes. After 17 minutes, sprinkle the remaining 30 g cheese on top and cook for the remaining 3 minutes, or until the cheese has melted, the eggs are set, and a toothpick inserted into the center comes out clean.
Serve the quiche warm or at room temperature.

## Tuna Patties with Spicy Sriracha Sauce

**Prep time: 10 minutes | Cook time: 10 minutes | Serves 4**

2 (170 g) cans tuna packed in oil, drained
3 tablespoons almond flour
2 tablespoons mayonnaise
1 teaspoon dried dill
½ teaspoon onion powder

Pinch of salt and pepper
Spicy Sriracha Sauce:
60 g mayonnaise
1 tablespoon Sriracha sauce
1 teaspoon garlic powder

Preheat the air fryer to 192ºC. Line the basket with baking paper.
In a large bowl, combine the tuna, almond flour, mayonnaise, dill, and onion powder. Season to taste with salt and freshly ground black pepper. Use a fork to stir, mashing with the back of the fork as necessary, until thoroughly combined.
Use an ice cream scoop to form the tuna mixture patties. Place the patties in a single layer on the baking paper in the air fryer basket. Press lightly with the bottom of the scoop to flatten into a circle about ½ inch thick. Pausing halfway through the cooking time to turn the patties, air fry for 10 minutes until lightly browned.
To make the Sriracha sauce: In a small bowl, combine the mayonnaise, Sriracha, and garlic powder. Serve the tuna patties topped with the Sriracha sauce.

## Panko-Crusted Fish Sticks

**Prep time: 10 minutes | Cook time: 15 minutes | Serves 4**

Tartar Sauce:
470 ml mayonnaise
2 tablespoons dill pickle relish
1 tablespoon dried minced onions
Fish Sticks:
Olive or vegetable oil, for spraying
455 g tilapia fillets

75 g plain flour
120 g panko bread crumbs
2 tablespoons Creole seasoning
2 teaspoons garlic granules
1 teaspoon onion powder
½ teaspoon salt
¼ teaspoon freshly ground black pepper
1 large egg

Make the Tartar Sauce:
In a small bowl, whisk together the mayonnaise, pickle relish, and onions.
Cover with plastic wrap and refrigerate until ready to serve. You can make this sauce ahead of time; the flavors will intensify as it chills. Make the Fish Sticks:
Preheat the air fryer to 176ºC. Line the air fryer basket with baking paper and spray lightly with oil.
Cut the fillets into equal-size sticks and place them in a zip-top plastic bag.
Add the flour to the bag, seal, and shake well until evenly coated.
In a shallow bowl, mix together the bread crumbs, Creole seasoning, garlic, onion powder, salt, and black pepper.
In a small bowl, whisk the egg.
Dip the fish sticks in the egg, then dredge in the bread crumb mixture until completely coated.
Place the fish sticks in the prepared basket. You may need to work in batches, depending on the size of your air fryer. Do not overcrowd. Spray lightly with oil.
Cook for 12 to 15 minutes, or until browned and cooked through. Serve with the tartar sauce.

## Creamy Haddock

**Prep time: 10 minutes | Cook time: 8 minutes | Serves 4**

455 g haddock fillet
1 teaspoon cayenne pepper
1 teaspoon salt

1 teaspoon coconut oil
120 ml heavy cream

Grease a baking pan with coconut oil.
Then put haddock fillet inside and sprinkle it with cayenne pepper, salt, and heavy cream. Put the baking pan in the air fryer basket and cook at 192ºC for 8 minutes.

## Parmesan Lobster Tails

**Prep time: 5 minutes | Cook time: 7 minutes | Serves 4**

4 (110 g) lobster tails
2 tablespoons salted butter, melted
1½ teaspoons Cajun seasoning, divided

¼ teaspoon salt
¼ teaspoon ground black pepper
40 g grated Parmesan cheese
15 g pork scratchings, finely crushed

Cut lobster tails open carefully with a pair of scissors and gently pull meat away from shells, resting meat on top of shells.
Brush lobster meat with butter and sprinkle with 1 teaspoon Cajun seasoning, ¼ teaspoon per tail.
In a small bowl, mix remaining Cajun seasoning, salt and pepper, Parmesan, and pork scratchings. Gently press ¼ mixture onto meat on each lobster tail.
Carefully place tails into ungreased air fryer basket. Adjust the temperature to 204ºC and air fry for 7 minutes. Lobster tails will be crispy and golden on top and have an internal temperature of at least 64ºC when done. Serve warm.

## Golden Beer-Battered Cod

**Prep time: 5 minutes | Cook time: 15 minutes | Serves 4**

2 eggs
240 ml malty beer
120 g plain flour
60 g corn flour

1 teaspoon garlic powder
Salt and pepper, to taste
4 cod fillets, 110 g each
Cooking spray

Preheat the air fryer to 204ºC.
In a shallow bowl, beat together the eggs with the beer. In another shallow bowl, thoroughly combine the flour and corn flour. Sprinkle with the garlic powder, salt, and pepper.
Dredge each cod fillet in the flour mixture, then in the egg mixture. Dip each piece of fish in the flour mixture a second time.
Spritz the air fryer basket with cooking spray. Arrange the cod fillets in the basket in a single layer.
Air fry in batches for 15 minutes until the cod reaches an internal temperature of 64ºC on a meat thermometer and the outside is crispy. Flip the fillets halfway through the cooking time.
Let the fish cool for 5 minutes and serve.

## Rainbow Salmon Kebabs

### Prep time: 10 minutes | Cook time: 8 minutes | Serves 2

170 g boneless, skinless salmon, cut into 1-inch cubes
¼ medium red onion, peeled and cut into 1-inch pieces
½ medium yellow bell pepper, seeded and cut into 1-inch
pieces
½ medium courgette, trimmed and cut into ½-inch slices
1 tablespoon olive oil
½ teaspoon salt
¼ teaspoon ground black pepper

Using one (6-inch) skewer, skewer 1 piece salmon, then 1 piece onion, 1 piece bell pepper, and finally 1 piece courgette. Repeat this pattern with additional skewers to make four kebabs total.
Drizzle with olive oil and sprinkle with salt and black pepper.
Place kebabs into ungreased air fryer basket. Adjust the temperature to 204ºC and air fry for 8 minutes, turning kebabs halfway through cooking. Salmon will easily flake and have an internal temperature of at least 64ºC when done; vegetables will be tender.
Serve warm.

## Firecracker Prawns

### Prep time: 10 minutes | Cook time: 7 minutes | Serves 4

455 g medium prawns, peeled and deveined
2 tablespoons salted butter, melted
½ teaspoon Old Bay seasoning
¼ teaspoon garlic powder
2 tablespoons Sriracha
¼ teaspoon powdered sweetener
60 ml full-fat mayonnaise
⅛ teaspoon ground black pepper

In a large bowl, toss prawns in butter, Old Bay seasoning, and garlic powder. Place prawns into the air fryer basket.
Adjust the temperature to 204ºC and set the timer for 7 minutes.
Flip the prawns halfway through the cooking time. Prawns will be bright pink when fully cooked.
In another large bowl, mix Sriracha, sweetener, mayonnaise, and pepper. Toss prawns in the spicy mixture and serve immediately.

## Cheesy Tuna Patties

### Prep time: 5 minutes | Cook time: 17 to 18 minutes | Serves 4

Tuna Patties:
455 g canned tuna, drained
1 egg, whisked
2 tablespoons shallots, minced
1 garlic clove, minced
1 cup grated Romano cheese
Sea salt and ground black
pepper, to taste
1 tablespoon sesame oil
Cheese Sauce:
1 tablespoon butter
240 ml beer
2 tablespoons grated Cheddar cheese

Mix together the canned tuna, whisked egg, shallots, garlic, cheese, salt, and pepper in a large bowl and stir to incorporate.
Divide the tuna mixture into four equal portions and form each portion into a patty with your hands. Refrigerate the patties for 2 hours.
When ready, brush both sides of each patty with sesame oil.
Preheat the air fryer to 182ºC.

Place the patties in the air fryer basket and bake for 14 minutes, flipping the patties halfway through, or until lightly browned and cooked through.
Meanwhile, melt the butter in a pan over medium heat.
Pour in the beer and whisk constantly, or until it begins to bubble.
Add the grated Colby cheese and mix well. Continue cooking for 3 to 4 minutes, or until the cheese melts.
Remove the patties from the basket to a plate. Drizzle them with the cheese sauce and serve immediately.

## Prawn and Cherry Tomato Kebabs

### Prep time: 15 minutes | Cook time: 5 minutes | Serves 4

680 g jumbo prawns, cleaned, peeled and deveined
455 g cherry tomatoes
2 tablespoons butter, melted
1 tablespoons Sriracha sauce
Sea salt and ground black pepper, to taste
1 teaspoon dried parsley flakes
½ teaspoon dried basil
½ teaspoon dried oregano
½ teaspoon mustard seeds
½ teaspoon marjoram
Special Equipment:
4 to 6 wooden skewers, soaked in water for 30 minutes

Preheat the air fryer to 204ºC.
Put all the ingredients in a large bowl and toss to coat well.
Make the kebabs: Thread, alternating jumbo prawns and cherry tomatoes, onto the wooden skewers that fit into the air fryer.
Arrange the kebabs in the air fryer basket. You may need to cook in batches depending on the size of your air fryer basket.
Air fry for 5 minutes, or until the prawns are pink and the cherry tomatoes are softened. Repeat with the remaining kebabs. Let the prawns and cherry tomato kebabs cool for 5 minutes and serve hot.

## Garlicky Cod Fillets

### Prep time: 10 minutes | Cook time: 10 to 12 minutes | Serves 4

1 teaspoon olive oil
4 cod fillets
¼ teaspoon fine sea salt
¼ teaspoon ground black pepper, or more to taste
1 teaspoon cayenne pepper
8 g fresh Italian parsley,
coarsely chopped
120 ml milk
1 Italian pepper, chopped
4 garlic cloves, minced
1 teaspoon dried basil
½ teaspoon dried oregano

Lightly coat the sides and bottom of a baking dish with the olive oil. Set aside.
In a large bowl, sprinkle the fillets with salt, black pepper, and cayenne pepper.
In a food processor, pulse the remaining ingredients until smoothly puréed.
Add the purée to the bowl of fillets and toss to coat, then transfer to the prepared baking dish.
Preheat the air fryer to 192ºC.
Put the baking dish in the air fryer basket and bake for 10 to 12 minutes, or until the fish flakes when pressed lightly with a fork.
Remove from the basket and serve warm.

# Crab Cakes with Lettuce and Apple Salad

**Prep time: 10 minutes | Cook time: 13 minutes | Serves 2**

230 g lump crab meat, picked over for shells
2 tablespoons panko bread crumbs
1 spring onions, minced
1 large egg
1 tablespoon mayonnaise
1½ teaspoons Dijon mustard
Pinch of cayenne pepper
2 shallots, sliced thin

1 tablespoon extra-virgin olive oil, divided
1 teaspoon lemon juice, plus lemon wedges for serving
⅛ teaspoon salt
Pinch of pepper
85 g small head round lettuce, torn into bite-size pieces
½ apple, cored and sliced thin

Preheat the air fryer to 204°C.

Line large plate with triple layer of paper towels. Transfer crab meat to prepared plate and pat dry with additional paper towels. Combine panko, spring onion, egg, mayonnaise, mustard, and cayenne in a bowl.

Using a rubber spatula, gently fold in crab meat until combined; discard paper towels. Divide crab mixture into 4 tightly packed balls, then flatten each into 1-inch-thick cake (cakes will be delicate). Transfer cakes to plate and refrigerate until firm, about 10 minutes.

Toss shallots with ½ teaspoon oil in separate bowl; transfer to air fryer basket. Air fry until shallots are browned, 5 to 7 minutes, tossing once halfway through cooking. Return shallots to now-empty bowl and set aside.

Arrange crab cakes in air fryer basket, spaced evenly apart. Return basket to air fryer and air fry until crab cakes are light golden brown on both sides, 8 to 10 minutes, flipping and rotating cakes halfway through cooking.

Meanwhile, whisk remaining 2½ teaspoons oil, lemon juice, salt, and pepper together in large bowl. Add lettuce, apple, and shallots and toss to coat. Serve crab cakes with salad, passing lemon wedges separately.

# Paprika Crab Burgers

**Prep time: 30 minutes | Cook time: 14 minutes | Serves 3**

2 eggs, beaten
1 shallot, chopped
2 garlic cloves, crushed
1 tablespoon olive oil
1 teaspoon yellow mustard
1 teaspoon fresh coriander,

chopped
280 g crab meat
1 teaspoon smoked paprika
½ teaspoon ground black pepper
Sea salt, to taste
70 g Parmesan cheese

In a mixing bowl, thoroughly combine the eggs, shallot, garlic, olive oil, mustard, coriander, crab meat, paprika, black pepper, and salt. Mix until well combined.

Shape the mixture into 6 patties. Roll the crab patties over grated Parmesan cheese, coating well on all sides. Place in your refrigerator for 2 hours.

Spritz the crab patties with cooking oil on both sides. Cook in the preheated air fryer at 182°C for 14 minutes. Serve on dinner rolls if desired. Bon appétit!

# Steamed Tuna with Lemongrass

**Prep time: 10 minutes | Cook time: 10 minutes | Serves 4**

4 small tuna steaks
2 tablespoons low-sodium soy sauce
2 teaspoons sesame oil
2 teaspoons rice wine vinegar
1 teaspoon grated peeled fresh

ginger
⅛ teaspoon freshly ground black pepper
1 stalk lemongrass, bent in half
3 tablespoons freshly squeezed lemon juice

Place the tuna steaks on a plate.

In a small bowl, whisk the soy sauce, sesame oil, vinegar, and ginger until combined. Pour this mixture over the tuna and gently rub it into both sides. Sprinkle the fish with the pepper. Let marinate for 10 minutes.

Insert the crisper plate into the basket and the basket into the unit. Preheat the unit to 200°C.

Once the unit is preheated, place the lemongrass into the basket and top it with the tuna steaks. Drizzle the tuna with the lemon juice and 1 tablespoon of water.

Cook for 10 minutes.

When the cooking is complete, a food thermometer inserted into the tuna should register at least 64°C. Discard the lemongrass and serve the tuna.

# Mackerel with Spinach

**Prep time: 15 minutes | Cook time: 20 minutes | Serves 5**

455 g mackerel, trimmed
1 bell pepper, chopped
15 g spinach, chopped

1 tablespoon avocado oil
1 teaspoon ground black pepper
1 teaspoon tomato paste

In the mixing bowl, mix bell pepper with spinach, ground black pepper, and tomato paste.

Fill the mackerel with spinach mixture.

Then brush the fish with avocado oil and put it in the air fryer.

Cook the fish at 185°C for 20 minutes.

# Simple Buttery Cod

**Prep time: 5 minutes | Cook time: 8 minutes | Serves 2**

2 cod fillets, 110 g each
2 tablespoons salted butter, melted

1 teaspoon Old Bay seasoning
½ medium lemon, sliced

Place cod fillets into a round baking dish. Brush each fillet with butter and sprinkle with Old Bay seasoning. Lay two lemon slices on each fillet. Cover the dish with foil and place into the air fryer basket.

Adjust the temperature to 176°C and bake for 8 minutes. Flip halfway through the cooking time. When cooked, internal temperature should be at least 64°C. Serve warm.

## Sole Fillets

**Prep time: 10 minutes | Cook time: 5 to 8 minutes | Serves 4**

1 egg white
1 tablespoon water
60 g panko breadcrumbs
2 tablespoons extra-light virgin olive oil

4 sole fillets, 110 g each
Salt and pepper, to taste
Olive or vegetable oil for misting or cooking spray

Preheat the air fryer to 390ºF (200ºC).
Beat together egg white and water in shallow dish.
In another shallow dish, mix panko crumbs and oil until well combined and crumbly (best done by hand).
Season sole fillets with salt and pepper to taste. Dip each fillet into egg mixture and then roll in panko crumbs, pressing in crumbs so that fish is nicely coated.
Spray the air fryer basket with nonstick cooking spray and add fillets. Air fry at 200ºC for 3 minutes.
Spray fish fillets but do not turn. Cook 2 to 5 minutes longer or until golden brown and crispy. Using a spatula, carefully remove fish from basket and serve.

## Tilapia Almondine

**Prep time: 10 minutes | Cook time: 10 minutes | Serves 2**

50 g almond flour or fine dried bread crumbs
2 tablespoons salted butter or ghee, melted
1 teaspoon black pepper
½ teaspoon kosher or coarse sea

salt
60 g mayonnaise
2 tilapia fillets
435 g thinly sliced almonds
Vegetable oil spray

In a small bowl, mix together the almond flour, butter, pepper and salt.
Spread the mayonnaise on both sides of each fish fillet. Dredge the fillets in the almond flour mixture. Spread the sliced almonds on one side of each fillet, pressing lightly to adhere.
Spray the air fryer basket with vegetable oil spray. Place the fish fillets in the basket. Set the air fryer to 164ºC for 10 minutes, or until the fish flakes easily with a fork.

## Snapper with Shallot and Tomato

**Prep time: 20 minutes | Cook time: 15 minutes | Serves 2**

2 snapper fillets
1 shallot, peeled and sliced
2 garlic cloves, halved
1 bell pepper, sliced
1 small-sized serrano pepper, sliced
1 tomato, sliced

1 tablespoon olive oil
¼ teaspoon freshly ground black pepper
½ teaspoon paprika
Sea salt, to taste
2 bay leaves

Place two baking paper sheets on a working surface. Place the fish in the center of one side of the baking paper.
Top with the shallot, garlic, peppers, and tomato. Drizzle olive oil

over the fish and vegetables. Season with black pepper, paprika, and salt. Add the bay leaves.
Fold over the other half of the baking paper. Now, fold the paper around the edges tightly and create a half moon shape, sealing the fish inside.
Cook in the preheated air fryer at 200ºC for 15 minutes.
Serve warm.

## Asian Marinated Salmon

**Prep time: 30 minutes | Cook time: 6 minutes | Serves 2**

Marinade:
60 ml wheat-free tamari or coconut aminos
2 tablespoons lime or lemon juice
2 tablespoons sesame oil
2 tablespoons powdered sweetener
2 teaspoons grated fresh ginger
2 cloves garlic, minced
½ teaspoon ground black pepper

2 (110 g) salmon fillets (about 1¼ inches thick)
Sliced spring onions, for garnish
Sauce (Optional):
60 ml beef stock
60 ml wheat-free tamari
3 tablespoons powdered sweetener
1 tablespoon tomato sauce
⅛ teaspoon guar gum or xanthan gum (optional, for thickening)

Make the marinade: In a medium-sized shallow dish, stir together all the ingredients for the marinade until well combined. Place the salmon in the marinade. Cover and refrigerate for at least 2 hours or overnight.
Preheat the air fryer to 204ºC.
Remove the salmon fillets from the marinade and place them in the air fryer, leaving space between them. Air fry for 6 minutes, or until the salmon is cooked through and flakes easily with a fork.
While the salmon cooks, make the sauce, if using: Place all the sauce ingredients except the guar gum in a medium-sized bowl and stir until well combined. Taste and adjust the sweetness to your liking. While whisking slowly, add the guar gum. Allow the sauce to thicken for 3 to 5 minutes. (The sauce can be made up to 3 days ahead and stored in an airtight container in the fridge.) Drizzle the sauce over the salmon before serving.
Garnish the salmon with sliced spring onions before serving. Store leftovers in an airtight container in the fridge for up to 3 days. Reheat in a preheated 176ºC air fryer for 3 minutes, or until heated through.

## Tuna Cakes

**Prep time: 10 minutes | Cook time: 10 minutes | Serves 4**

4 (85 g) tuna fillets, drained
1 large egg, whisked
2 tablespoons peeled and

chopped white onion
½ teaspoon Old Bay seasoning

In a large bowl, mix all ingredients together and form into four patties.
Place patties into ungreased air fryer basket. Adjust the temperature to 204ºC and air fry for 10 minutes. Patties will be browned and crispy when done.
Let cool 5 minutes before serving.

# Crispy Fish Sticks

**Prep time: 15 minutes | Cook time: 10 minutes | Serves 4**

30 g crushed panko breadcrumbs
25 g blanched finely ground almond flour
½ teaspoon Old Bay seasoning

1 tablespoon coconut oil
1 large egg
455 g cod fillet, cut into ¾-inch strips

Place panko, almond flour, Old Bay seasoning, and coconut oil into a large bowl and mix together. In a medium bowl, whisk egg.
Dip each fish stick into the egg and then gently press into the flour mixture, coating as fully and evenly as possible. Place fish sticks into the air fryer basket.
Adjust the temperature to 204ºC and air fry for 10 minutes or until golden.
Serve immediately.

# Cilantro Lime Baked Salmon

**Prep time: 10 minutes | Cook time: 12 minutes | Serves 2**

2 salmon fillets, 85 g each, skin removed
1 tablespoon salted butter, melted
1 teaspoon chilli powder

½ teaspoon finely minced garlic
20 g sliced pickled jalapeños
½ medium lime, juiced
2 tablespoons chopped coriander

Place salmon fillets into a round baking pan. Brush each with butter and sprinkle with chilli powder and garlic.
Place jalapeño slices on top and around salmon. Pour half of the lime juice over the salmon and cover with foil. Place pan into the air fryer basket.
Adjust the temperature to 188ºC and bake for 12 minutes.
When fully cooked, salmon should flake easily with a fork and reach an internal temperature of at least 64ºC.
To serve, spritz with remaining lime juice and garnish with coriander.

# Cod with Creamy Mustard Sauce

**Prep time: 10 minutes | Cook time: 10 minutes | Serves 4**

Fish:
Olive or vegetable oil, for spraying
455 g cod fillets
2 tablespoons olive oil
1 tablespoon lemon juice
1 teaspoon salt

½ teaspoon freshly ground black pepper
Mustard Sauce:
120 ml heavy cream
3 tablespoons Dijon mustard
1 tablespoon unsalted butter
1 teaspoon salt

Make the Fish:
Line the air fryer basket with baking paper and spray lightly with oil.
Rub the cod with the olive oil and lemon juice. Season with the salt and black pepper.
Place the cod in the prepared basket. You may need to work in batches, depending on the size of your air fryer.
Roast at 176ºC for 5 minutes. Increase the temperature to 204ºC and cook for another 5 minutes, until flaky and the internal temperature reaches 64ºC. Make the Mustard Sauce:
In a small saucepan, mix together the heavy cream, mustard, butter, and salt and bring to a simmer over low heat. Cook for 3 to 4 minutes, or until the sauce starts to thicken.
Transfer the cod to a serving plate and drizzle with the mustard sauce. Serve immediately.

# Smoky Prawns and Chorizo Tapas

**Prep time: 15 minutes | Cook time: 10 minutes | Serves 2 to 4**

110 g Spanish (cured) chorizo, halved horizontally and sliced crosswise
230 g raw medium prawns, peeled and deveined
1 tablespoon extra-virgin olive oil
1 small shallot, halved and thinly sliced
1 garlic clove, minced

1 tablespoon finely chopped fresh oregano
½ teaspoon smoked Spanish paprika
¼ teaspoon kosher or coarse sea salt
¼ teaspoon black pepper
3 tablespoons fresh orange juice
1 tablespoon minced fresh parsley

Place the chorizo in a baking pan. Set the pan in the air fryer basket. Set the air fryer to 192ºC for 5 minutes, or until the chorizo has started to brown and render its fat.
Meanwhile, in a large bowl, combine the prawns, olive oil, shallot, garlic, oregano, paprika, salt, and pepper. Toss until the prawns are well coated.
Transfer the prawns to the pan with the chorizo. Stir to combine. Place the pan in the air fryer basket. Cook for 10 minutes, stirring halfway through the cooking time.
Transfer the prawns and chorizo to a serving dish. Drizzle with the orange juice and toss to combine. Sprinkle with the parsley.

# Seasoned Breaded Prawns

**Prep time: 15 minutes | Cook time: 10 to 15 minutes | Serves 4**

2 teaspoons Old Bay seasoning, divided
½ teaspoon garlic powder
½ teaspoon onion powder
455 g large prawns, peeled and

deveined, with tails on
2 large eggs
75 g whole-wheat panko bread crumbs
Cooking spray

Preheat the air fryer to 192ºC.
Spray the air fryer basket lightly with cooking spray.
In a medium bowl, mix together 1 teaspoon of Old Bay seasoning, garlic powder, and onion powder. Add the prawns and toss with the seasoning mix to lightly coat.
In a separate small bowl, whisk the eggs with 1 teaspoon water.
In a shallow bowl, mix together the remaining 1 teaspoon Old Bay seasoning and the panko bread crumbs.
Dip each prawns in the egg mixture and dredge in the bread crumb mixture to evenly coat.
Place the prawns in the air fryer basket, in a single layer. Lightly spray the prawns with cooking spray. You many need to cook the prawns in batches.

# Chapter 7 Vegetables and Sides

# Chapter 7 Vegetables and Sides

## Burger Bun for One

**Prep time: 2 minutes | Cook time: 5 minutes | Serves 1**

2 tablespoons salted butter, melted
25 g blanched finely ground almond flour
¼ teaspoon baking powder
⅛ teaspoon apple cider vinegar
1 large egg, whisked

Pour butter into an ungreased ramekin. Add flour, baking powder, and vinegar to ramekin and stir until combined. Add egg and stir until batter is mostly smooth.
Place ramekin into air fryer basket. Adjust the temperature to 180°C and bake for 5 minutes. When done, the centre will be firm and the top slightly browned.
Let cool, about 5 minutes, then remove from ramekin and slice in half. Serve.

## Parsnip Fries with Romesco Sauce

**Prep time: 20 minutes | Cook time: 24 minutes | Serves 4**

Romesco Sauce:
1 red pepper, halved and seeded
1 (1-inch) thick slice of Italian bread, torn into pieces
130 g almonds, toasted
Olive oil
½ Jalapeño pepper, seeded
1 tablespoon fresh parsley leaves
1 clove garlic
2 plum tomatoes, peeled and
seeded
1 tablespoon red wine vinegar
¼ teaspoon smoked paprika
½ teaspoon salt
180 ml olive oil
3 parsnips, peeled and cut into long strips
2 teaspoons olive oil
Salt and freshly ground black pepper, to taste

Preheat the air fryer to 200°C.
Place the red pepper halves, cut side down, in the air fryer basket and air fry for 8 to 10 minutes, or until the skin turns black all over. Remove the pepper from the air fryer and let it cool. When it is cool enough to handle, peel the pepper.
Toss the torn bread and almonds with a little olive oil and air fry for 4 minutes, shaking the basket a couple times throughout the cooking time. When the bread and almonds are nicely toasted, remove them from the air fryer and let them cool for just a minute or two.
Combine the toasted bread, almonds, roasted red pepper, Jalapeño pepper, parsley, garlic, tomatoes, vinegar, smoked paprika and salt in a food processor or blender. Process until smooth. With the processor running, add the olive oil through the feed tube until the sauce comes together in a smooth paste that is barely pourable.
Toss the parsnip strips with the olive oil, salt and freshly ground black pepper and air fry at 200°C for 10 minutes, shaking the basket a couple times during the cooking process so they brown and cook evenly. Serve the parsnip fries warm with the Romesco sauce to dip into.

## Rosemary New Potatoes

**Prep time: 10 minutes | Cook time: 5 to 6 minutes | Serves 4**

3 large red potatoes
¼ teaspoon ground rosemary
¼ teaspoon ground thyme
⅛ teaspoon salt
⅛ teaspoon ground black pepper
2 teaspoons extra-light olive oil

Preheat the air fryer to 170°C. Place potatoes in large bowl and sprinkle with rosemary, thyme, salt, and pepper.
Stir with a spoon to distribute seasonings evenly.
Add oil to potatoes and stir again to coat well.
Air fry at 170°C for 4 minutes. Stir and break apart any that have stuck together.
Cook an additional 1 to 2 minutes or until fork-tender.

## Balsamic Brussels Sprouts

**Prep time: 5 minutes | Cook time: 12 minutes | Serves 4**

180 g trimmed and halved fresh Brussels sprouts
2 tablespoons olive oil
¼ teaspoon salt
¼ teaspoon ground black pepper
2 tablespoons balsamic vinegar
2 slices cooked sugar-free bacon, crumbled

In a large bowl, toss Brussels sprouts in olive oil, then sprinkle with salt and pepper.
Place into ungreased air fryer basket. Adjust the temperature to 192°C and set the timer for 12 minutes, shaking the basket halfway through cooking. Brussels sprouts will be tender and browned when done.
Place sprouts in a large serving dish and drizzle with balsamic vinegar. Sprinkle bacon over top.
Serve warm.

## Rosemary-Roasted Red Potatoes

**Prep time: 5 minutes | Cook time: 20 minutes | Serves 6**

450 g red potatoes, quartered
65 ml olive oil
½ teaspoon coarse sea salt
¼ teaspoon black pepper
1 garlic clove, minced
4 rosemary sprigs

Preheat the air fryer to 180°C.
In a large bowl, toss the potatoes with the olive oil, salt, pepper, and garlic until well coated.
Pour the potatoes into the air fryer basket and top with the sprigs of rosemary.
Roast for 10 minutes, then stir or toss the potatoes and roast for 10 minutes more.
Remove the rosemary sprigs and serve the potatoes. Season with additional salt and pepper, if needed.

## Cheese-Walnut Stuffed Mushrooms

**Prep time: 5 minutes | Cook time: 10 minutes | Serves 4**

| | |
|---|---|
| 4 large portobello mushrooms | 35 g minced walnuts |
| 1 tablespoon rapeseed oil | 2 tablespoons chopped fresh |
| 110 g shredded Mozzarella | parsley |
| cheese | Cooking spray |

Preheat the air fryer to 180°C. Spritz the air fryer basket with cooking spray.

On a clean work surface, remove the mushroom stems. Scoop out the gills with a spoon and discard. Coat the mushrooms with rapeseed oil. Top each mushroom evenly with the shredded Mozzarella cheese, followed by the minced walnuts.

Arrange the mushrooms in the air fryer and roast for 10 minutes until golden brown.

Transfer the mushrooms to a plate and sprinkle the parsley on top for garnish before serving.

## Lush Vegetable Salad

**Prep time: 15 minutes | Cook time: 10 minutes | Serves 4**

| | |
|---|---|
| 6 plum tomatoes, halved | oil |
| 2 large red onions, sliced | 1 teaspoon paprika |
| 4 long red pepper, sliced | ½ lemon, juiced |
| 2 yellow pepper, sliced | Salt and ground black pepper, to |
| 6 cloves garlic, crushed | taste |
| 1 tablespoon extra-virgin olive | 1 tablespoon baby capers |

Preheat the air fryer to 220°C.

Put the tomatoes, onions, peppers, and garlic in a large bowl and cover with the extra-virgin olive oil, paprika, and lemon juice. Sprinkle with salt and pepper as desired.

Line the inside of the air fryer basket with aluminum foil. Put the vegetables inside and air fry for 10 minutes, ensuring the edges turn brown.

Serve in a salad bowl with the baby capers.

## Caesar Whole Cauliflower

**Prep time: 20 minutes | Cook time: 30 minutes | Serves 2 to 4**

| | |
|---|---|
| 3 tablespoons olive oil | drained and finely minced |
| 2 tablespoons red wine vinegar | coarse sea salt and freshly |
| 2 tablespoons Worcestershire | ground black pepper, to taste |
| sauce | 1 small head cauliflower (about |
| 2 tablespoons grated Parmesan | 450 g), green leaves trimmed |
| cheese | and stem trimmed flush with the |
| 1 tablespoon Dijon mustard | bottom of the head |
| 4 garlic cloves, minced | 1 tablespoon roughly chopped |
| 4 oil-packed anchovy fillets, | fresh flat-leaf parsley (optional) |

In a liquid measuring jug, whisk together the olive oil, vinegar, Worcestershire, Parmesan, mustard, garlic, anchovies, and salt and pepper to taste. Place the cauliflower head upside down on a cutting board and use a paring knife to make an "x" through the full length

of the core.

Transfer the cauliflower head to a large bowl and pour half the dressing over it. Turn the cauliflower head to coat it in the dressing, then let it rest, stem-side up, in the dressing for at least 10 minutes and up to 30 minutes to allow the dressing to seep into all its nooks and crannies.

Transfer the cauliflower head, stem-side down, to the air fryer and air fry at 170°C or 25 minutes. Drizzle the remaining dressing over the cauliflower and air fry at 200°C until the top of the cauliflower is golden brown and the core is tender, about 5 minutes more.

Remove the basket from the air fryer and transfer the cauliflower to a large plate. Sprinkle with the parsley, if you like, and serve hot.

## Citrus Sweet Potatoes and Carrots

**Prep time: 5 minutes | Cook time: 20 to 25 minutes | Serves 4**

| | |
|---|---|
| 2 large carrots, cut into 1-inch | 2 garlic cloves, minced |
| chunks | 2 tablespoons honey |
| 1 medium sweet potato, peeled | 1 tablespoon freshly squeezed |
| and cut into 1-inch cubes | orange juice |
| 25 g chopped onion | 2 teaspoons butter, melted |

Insert the crisper plate into the basket and the basket into the unit. Preheat the unit by selecting AIR ROAST, setting the temperature to 200°C, and setting the time to 3 minutes. Select START/STOP to begin.

In a 6-by-2-inch round pan, toss together the carrots, sweet potato, onion, garlic, honey, orange juice, and melted butter to coat.

Once the unit is preheated, place the pan into the basket.

Select AIR ROAST, set the temperature to 200°C, and set the time to 25 minutes. Select START/STOP to begin.

After 15 minutes, remove the basket and shake the vegetables. Reinsert the basket to resume cooking. After 5 minutes, if the vegetables are tender and glazed, they are done. If not, resume cooking.

When the cooking is complete, serve immediately.

## Tofu Bites

**Prep time: 15 minutes | Cook time: 30 minutes | Serves 4**

| | |
|---|---|
| 1 packaged firm tofu, cubed and | 1 teaspoon hot sauce |
| pressed to remove excess water | 2 tablespoons sesame seeds |
| 1 tablespoon soy sauce | 1 teaspoon garlic powder |
| 1 tablespoon ketchup | Salt and ground black pepper, to |
| 1 tablespoon maple syrup | taste |
| ½ teaspoon vinegar | Cooking spray |
| 1 teaspoon liquid smoke | |

Preheat the air fryer to 192°C.

Spritz a baking dish with cooking spray.

Combine all the ingredients to coat the tofu completely and allow the marinade to absorb for half an hour.

Transfer the tofu to the baking dish, then air fry for 15 minutes. Flip the tofu over and air fry for another 15 minutes on the other side.

Serve immediately.

# Herbed Shiitake Mushrooms

**Prep time: 10 minutes | Cook time: 5 minutes | Serves 4**

230 g shiitake mushrooms, stems removed and caps roughly chopped
1 tablespoon olive oil
½ teaspoon salt
Freshly ground black pepper, to taste
1 teaspoon chopped fresh thyme leaves
1 teaspoon chopped fresh oregano
1 tablespoon chopped fresh parsley

Preheat the air fryer to 200ºC.
Toss the mushrooms with the olive oil, salt, pepper, thyme and oregano.
Air fry for 5 minutes, shaking the basket once or twice during the cooking process. The mushrooms will still be somewhat chewy with a meaty texture. If you'd like them a little more tender, add a couple of minutes to this cooking time.
Once cooked, add the parsley to the mushrooms and toss. Season again to taste and serve.

# Mushrooms with Goat Cheese

**Prep time: 10 minutes | Cook time: 10 minutes | Serves 4**

3 tablespoons vegetable oil
450 g mixed mushrooms, trimmed and sliced
1 clove garlic, minced
¼ teaspoon dried thyme
½ teaspoon black pepper
110 g goat cheese, diced
2 teaspoons chopped fresh thyme leaves (optional)

In a baking pan, combine the oil, mushrooms, garlic, dried thyme, and pepper. Stir in the goat cheese.
Place the pan in the air fryer basket. Set the air fryer to 200ºC for 10 minutes, stirring halfway through the cooking time.
Sprinkle with fresh thyme, if desired.

# Ricotta Potatoes

**Prep time: 15 minutes | Cook time: 15 minutes | Serves 4**

4 potatoes
2 tablespoons olive oil
110 g Ricotta cheese, at room temperature
2 tablespoons chopped spring onions
1 tablespoon roughly chopped
fresh parsley
1 tablespoon minced coriander
60 g Cheddar cheese, preferably freshly grated
1 teaspoon celery seeds
½ teaspoon salt
½ teaspoon garlic pepper

Preheat the air fryer to 180ºC.
Pierce the skin of the potatoes with a knife.
Air fry in the air fryer basket for 13 minutes. If they are not cooked through by this time, leave for 2 to 3 minutes longer.
In the meantime, make the stuffing by combining all the other ingredients.
Cut halfway into the cooked potatoes to open them.
Spoon equal amounts of the stuffing into each potato and serve hot.

# "Faux-Tato" Hash

**Prep time: 10 minutes | Cook time: 12 minutes | Serves 4**

450 g radishes, ends removed, quartered
¼ medium yellow onion, peeled and diced
½ medium green pepper, seeded
and chopped
2 tablespoons salted butter, melted
½ teaspoon garlic powder
¼ teaspoon ground black pepper

In a large bowl, combine radishes, onion, and bell pepper. Toss with butter.
Sprinkle garlic powder and black pepper over mixture in bowl, then spoon into ungreased air fryer basket.
Adjust the temperature to 160ºC and air fry for 12 minutes. Shake basket halfway through cooking. Radishes will be tender when done.
Serve warm.

# Broccoli with Sesame Dressing

**Prep time: 5 minutes | Cook time: 10 minutes | Serves 4**

425 g broccoli florets, cut into bite-size pieces
1 tablespoon olive oil
¼ teaspoon salt
2 tablespoons sesame seeds
2 tablespoons rice vinegar
2 tablespoons coconut aminos
2 tablespoons sesame oil
½ teaspoon xylitol
¼ teaspoon red pepper flakes (optional)

Preheat the air fryer to 200ºC.
In a large bowl, toss the broccoli with the olive oil and salt until thoroughly coated.
Transfer the broccoli to the air fryer basket. Pausing halfway through the cooking time to shake the basket, air fry for 10 minutes until the stems are tender and the edges are beginning to crisp.
Meanwhile, in the same large bowl, whisk together the sesame seeds, vinegar, coconut aminos, sesame oil, xylitol, and red pepper flakes (if using).
Transfer the broccoli to the bowl and toss until thoroughly coated with the seasonings.
Serve warm or at room temperature.

# Garlic Courgette and Red Peppers

**Prep time: 5 minutes | Cook time: 15 minutes | Serves 6**

2 medium courgette, cubed
1 red pepper, diced
2 garlic cloves, sliced
2 tablespoons olive oil
½ teaspoon salt

Preheat the air fryer to 193ºC.
In a large bowl, mix together the courgette, bell pepper, and garlic with the olive oil and salt.
Pour the mixture into the air fryer basket, and roast for 7 minutes. Shake or stir, then roast for 7 to 8 minutes more.

## Gold Artichoke Hearts

**Prep time: 15 minutes | Cook time: 8 minutes | Serves 4**

12 whole artichoke hearts
packed in water, drained
60 g plain flour
1 egg

40 g panko bread crumbs
1 teaspoon Italian seasoning
Cooking oil spray

Squeeze any excess water from the artichoke hearts and place them on paper towels to dry.
Place the flour in a small bowl.
In another small bowl, beat the egg.
In a third small bowl, stir together the panko and Italian seasoning.
Dip the artichoke hearts in the flour, in the egg, and into the panko mixture until coated.
Insert the crisper plate into the basket and the basket into the unit. Preheat the unit by selecting AIR FRY, setting the temperature to 192ºC, and setting the time to 3 minutes. Select START/STOP to begin.
Once the unit is preheated, spray the crisper plate and the basket with cooking oil. Place the breaded artichoke hearts into the basket, stacking them if needed.
Select AIR FRY, set the temperature to 192ºC, and set the time to 8 minutes. Select START/STOP to begin.
After 4 minutes, use tongs to flip the artichoke hearts. I recommend flipping instead of shaking because the hearts are small, and this will help keep the breading intact. Re-insert the basket to resume cooking.1When the cooking is complete, the artichoke hearts should be deep golden brown and crisp. Cool for 5 minutes before serving.

## Lemony Broccoli

**Prep time: 10 minutes | Cook time: 9 to 14 minutes per batch | Serves 4**

1 large head broccoli, rinsed and
patted dry
2 teaspoons extra-virgin olive
oil

1 tablespoon freshly squeezed
lemon juice
Olive oil spray

Cut off the broccoli florets and separate them. You can use the stems, too; peel the stems and cut them into 1-inch chunks.
Insert the crisper plate into the basket and the basket into the unit. Preheat the unit by selecting AIR ROAST, setting the temperature to 200ºC, and setting the time to 3 minutes. Select START/STOP to begin.
In a large bowl, toss together the broccoli, olive oil, and lemon juice until coated.
Once the unit is preheated, spray the crisper plate with olive oil. Working in batches, place half the broccoli into the basket.
Select AIR ROAST, set the temperature to 200ºC, and set the time to 14 minutes. Select START/STOP to begin.
After 5 minutes, remove the basket and shake the broccoli. Reinsert the basket to resume cooking. Check the broccoli after 5 minutes. If it is crisp-tender and slightly brown around the edges, it is done. If not, resume cooking.
When the cooking is complete, transfer the broccoli to a serving bowl. Repeat steps 5 and 6 with the remaining broccoli. Serve immediately.

## Citrus-Roasted Broccoli Florets

**Prep time: 5 minutes | Cook time: 12 minutes | Serves 6**

285 g broccoli florets
(approximately 1 large head)
2 tablespoons olive oil
½ teaspoon salt

130 ml orange juice
1 tablespoon raw honey
Orange wedges, for serving
(optional)

Preheat the air fryer to 180ºC.
In a large bowl, combine the broccoli, olive oil, salt, orange juice, and honey. Toss the broccoli in the liquid until well coated.
Pour the broccoli mixture into the air fryer basket and roast for 6 minutes. Stir and roast for 6 minutes more.
Serve alone or with orange wedges for additional citrus flavour, if desired.

## Butternut Squash Croquettes

**Prep time: 5 minutes | Cook time: 17 minutes | Serves 4**

⅓ butternut squash, peeled and
grated
40 g plain flour
2 eggs, whisked
4 cloves garlic, minced
1½ tablespoons olive oil

1 teaspoon fine sea salt
⅓ teaspoon freshly ground
black pepper, or more to taste
⅓ teaspoon dried sage
A pinch of ground allspice

Preheat the air fryer to 170ºC. Line the air fryer basket with parchment paper.
In a mixing bowl, stir together all the ingredients until well combined.
Make the squash croquettes: Use a small cookie scoop to drop tablespoonfuls of the squash mixture onto a lightly floured surface and shape into balls with your hands. Transfer them to the air fryer basket.
Air fry for 17 minutes until the squash croquettes are golden brown. Remove from the basket to a plate and serve warm.

## Zesty Fried Asparagus

**Prep time: 3 minutes | Cook time: 10 minutes | Serves 4**

Oil, for spraying
10 to 12 spears asparagus,
trimmed
2 tablespoons olive oil

1 tablespoon garlic powder
1 teaspoon chili powder
½ teaspoon ground cumin
¼ teaspoon salt

Line the air fryer basket with parchment and spray lightly with oil.
If the asparagus are too long to fit easily in the air fryer, cut them in half.
Place the asparagus, olive oil, garlic, chili powder, cumin, and salt in a zip-top plastic bag, seal, and toss until evenly coated.
Place the asparagus in the prepared basket.
Roast at 200ºC for 5 minutes, flip, and cook for another 5 minutes, or until bright green and firm but tender.

## Southwestern Roasted Corn

### Prep time: 10 minutes | Cook time: 10 minutes | Serves 4

Corn:
240 g thawed frozen corn kernels
50 g diced yellow onion
150 g mixed diced bell peppers
1 jalapeño, diced
1 tablespoon fresh lemon juice
1 teaspoon ground cumin
½ teaspoon ancho chili powder
½ teaspoon coarse sea salt
For Serving:
150 g queso fresco or feta cheese
10 g chopped fresh coriander
1 tablespoon fresh lemon juice

For the corn: In a large bowl, stir together the corn, onion, bell peppers, jalapeño, lemon juice, cumin, chili powder, and salt until well incorporated.
Pour the spiced vegetables into the air fryer basket. Set the air fryer to 192ºC for 10 minutes, stirring halfway through the cooking time.
Transfer the corn mixture to a serving bowl. Add the cheese, coriander, and lemon juice and stir well to combine. Serve immediately.

## Green Peas with Mint

### Prep time: 5 minutes | Cook time: 5 minutes | Serves 4

75 g shredded lettuce
1 (280 g) package frozen green peas, thawed
1 tablespoon fresh mint, shredded
1 teaspoon melted butter

Lay the shredded lettuce in the air fryer basket.
Toss together the peas, mint, and melted butter and spoon over the lettuce.
Air fry at 180ºC for 5 minutes, until peas are warm and lettuce wilts.

## Buffalo Cauliflower with Blue Cheese

### Prep time: 15 minutes | Cook time: 5 to 7 minutes per batch | Serves 6

1 large head cauliflower, rinsed and separated into small florets
1 tablespoon extra-virgin olive oil
½ teaspoon garlic powder
Cooking oil spray
80 ml hot wing sauce
190 g nonfat Greek yogurt
60 g buttermilk
½ teaspoon hot sauce
1 celery stalk, chopped
2 tablespoons crumbled blue cheese

Insert the crisper plate into the basket and the basket into the unit. Preheat the unit by selecting AIR FRY, setting the temperature to192ºC, and setting the time to 3 minutes. Select START/STOP to begin.
In a large bowl, toss together the cauliflower florets and olive oil. Sprinkle with the garlic powder and toss again to coat.
Once the unit is preheated, spray the crisper plate with cooking oil. Put half the cauliflower into the basket.
Select AIR FRY, set the temperature to192ºC, and set the time to 7 minutes. Select START/STOP to begin.

After 3 minutes, remove the basket and shake the cauliflower. Reinsert the basket to resume cooking. After 2 minutes, check the cauliflower. It is done when it is browned. If not, resume cooking. When the cooking is complete, transfer the cauliflower to a serving bowl and toss with half the hot wing sauce.
Repeat steps 4, 5, and 6 with the remaining cauliflower and hot wing sauce.
In a small bowl, stir together the yogurt, buttermilk, hot sauce, celery, and blue cheese. Drizzle the sauce over the finished cauliflower and serve.

## Garlic Roasted Broccoli

### Prep time: 8 minutes | Cook time: 10 to 14 minutes | Serves 6

1 head broccoli, cut into bite-size florets
1 tablespoon avocado oil
2 teaspoons minced garlic
⅛ teaspoon red pepper flakes
Sea salt and freshly ground black pepper, to taste
1 tablespoon freshly squeezed lemon juice
½ teaspoon lemon zest

In a large bowl, toss together the broccoli, avocado oil, garlic, red pepper flakes, salt, and pepper.
Set the air fryer to 192ºC. Arrange the broccoli in a single layer in the air fryer basket, working in batches if necessary. Roast for 10 to 14 minutes, until the broccoli is lightly charred.
Place the florets in a medium bowl and toss with the lemon juice and lemon zest. Serve.

## Buttery Mushrooms

### Prep time: 10 minutes | Cook time: 10 minutes | Serves 4

230 g shitake mushrooms, halved
2 tablespoons salted butter,
melted
¼ teaspoon salt
¼ teaspoon ground black pepper

In a medium bowl, toss mushrooms with butter, then sprinkle with salt and pepper. Place into ungreased air fryer basket.
Adjust the temperature to 200ºC and air fry for 10 minutes, shaking the basket halfway through cooking. Mushrooms will be tender when done.
Serve warm.

## Crispy Chickpeas

### Prep time: 5 minutes | Cook time: 15 minutes | Serves 4

1 (425 g) can chickpeas, drained but not rinsed
2 tablespoons olive oil
1 teaspoon salt
2 tablespoons lemon juice

Preheat the air fryer to 200ºC.
Add all the ingredients together in a bowl and mix. Transfer this mixture to the air fryer basket.
Air fry for 15 minutes, ensuring the chickpeas become nice and crispy.
Serve immediately.

# Roasted Brussels Sprouts with Bacon

**Prep time: 10 minutes | Cook time: 20 minutes | Serves 4**

4 slices thick-cut bacon, chopped (about 110 g)
450 g Brussels sprouts, halved (or quartered if large)

Freshly ground black pepper, to taste

Preheat the air fryer to 192°C.
Air fry the bacon for 5 minutes, shaking the basket once or twice during the cooking time.
Add the Brussels sprouts to the basket and drizzle a little bacon fat from the bottom of the air fryer drawer into the basket.
Toss the sprouts to coat with the bacon fat. Air fry for an additional 15 minutes, or until the Brussels sprouts are tender to a knifepoint.
Season with freshly ground black pepper.

# Sesame Taj Tofu

**Prep time: 5 minutes | Cook time: 25 minutes | Serves 4**

1 block firm tofu, pressed and cut into 1-inch thick cubes
2 tablespoons soy sauce
2 teaspoons toasted sesame seeds

1 teaspoon rice vinegar
1 tablespoon corn flour

Preheat the air fryer to 200°C.
Add the tofu, soy sauce, sesame seeds, and rice vinegar in a bowl together and mix well to coat the tofu cubes. Then cover the tofu in corn flour and put it in the air fryer basket.
Air fry for 25 minutes, giving the basket a shake at five-minute intervals to ensure the tofu cooks evenly.
Serve immediately.

# Bacon Potatoes and Green Beans

**Prep time: 10 minutes | Cook time: 25 minutes | Serves 4**

Oil, for spraying
900 g medium Maris Piper potatoes, quartered
100 g bacon bits

280 g fresh green beans
1 teaspoon salt
½ teaspoon freshly ground black pepper

Line the air fryer basket with parchment and spray lightly with oil.
Place the potatoes in the prepared basket.
Top with the bacon bits and green beans. Sprinkle with the salt and black pepper and spray liberally with oil.
Air fry at 180°C for 25 minutes, stirring after 12 minutes and spraying with oil, until the potatoes are easily pierced with a fork.

# Chapter 8 Snacks and Appetizers

# Chapter 8 Snacks and Appetizers

## Courgette Feta Roulades

**Prep time: 10 minutes | Cook time: 10 minutes | Serves 6**

120 ml feta
1 garlic clove, minced
2 tablespoons fresh basil, minced
1 tablespoon capers, minced

⅛ teaspoon salt
⅛ teaspoon red pepper flakes
1 tablespoon lemon juice
2 medium courgette
12 toothpicks

Preheat the air fryer to 182°C. (If using a grill attachment, make sure it is inside the air fryer during preheating.)
In a small bowl, combine the feta, garlic, basil, capers, salt, red pepper flakes, and lemon juice.
Slice the courgette into ⅛-inch strips lengthwise. (Each courgette should yield around 6 strips.)
Spread 1 tablespoon of the cheese filling onto each slice of courgette, then roll it up and secure it with a toothpick through the middle.
Place the courgette roulades into the air fryer basket in a single layer, making sure that they don't touch each other.
Bake or grill in the air fryer for 10 minutes.
Remove the courgette roulades from the air fryer and gently remove the toothpicks before serving.

## Courgette Fries with Roasted Garlic Aioli

**Prep time: 20 minutes | Cook time: 12 minutes | Serves 4**

1 tablespoon vegetable oil
½ head green or savoy cabbage, finely shredded
Roasted Garlic Aioli:
1 teaspoon roasted garlic
120 ml mayonnaise
2 tablespoons olive oil
Juice of ½ lemon
Salt and pepper, to taste

Courgette Fries:
120 ml flour
2 eggs, beaten
240 ml seasoned breadcrumbs
Salt and pepper, to taste
1 large courgette, cut into ½-inch sticks
Olive oil

Make the aioli: Combine the roasted garlic, mayonnaise, olive oil and lemon juice in a bowl and whisk well. Season the aioli with salt and pepper to taste.
Prepare the courgette fries. Create a dredging station with three shallow dishes. Place the flour in the first shallow dish and season well with salt and freshly ground black pepper. Put the beaten eggs in the second shallow dish.
In the third shallow dish, combine the breadcrumbs, salt and pepper. Dredge the courgette sticks, coating with flour first, then dipping them into the eggs to coat, and finally tossing in breadcrumbs.
Shake the dish with the breadcrumbs and pat the crumbs onto the courgette sticks gently with your hands, so they stick evenly.
Place the courgette fries on a flat surface and let them sit at least 10 minutes before air frying to let them dry out a little. Preheat the air fryer to 204°C.
Spray the courgette sticks with olive oil and place them into the air fryer basket. You can air fry the courgette in two layers, placing the second layer in the opposite direction to the first.
Air fry for 12 minutes turning and rotating the fries halfway through the cooking time. Spray with additional oil when you turn them over.
Serve courgette fries warm with the roasted garlic aioli.

## Veggie Salmon Nachos

**Prep time: 10 minutes | Cook time: 9 to 12 minutes | Serves 6**

57 g baked no-salt corn tortilla chips
1 (142 g) baked salmon fillet, flaked
120 ml canned low-salt black beans, rinsed and drained

1 red pepper, chopped
120 ml grated carrot
1 jalapeño pepper, minced
80 ml shredded low-salt low-fat Swiss cheese
1 tomato, chopped

Preheat the air fryer to 182°C.
In a baking pan, layer the tortilla chips. Top with the salmon, black beans, red pepper, carrot, jalapeño, and Swiss cheese.
Bake in the air fryer for 9 to 12 minutes, or until the cheese is melted and starts to brown.
Top with the tomato and serve.

## Caramelized Onion Dip with White Cheese

**Prep time: 5 minutes | Cook time: 30 minutes | Serves 8 to 10**

1 tablespoon butter
1 medium onion, halved and thinly sliced
¼ teaspoon rock salt, plus additional for seasoning
113 g soft white cheese
120 ml sour cream

¼ teaspoon onion powder
1 tablespoon chopped fresh chives
Black pepper, to taste
Thick-cut potato crisps or vegetable crisps

Place the butter in a baking pan. Place the pan in the air fryer basket. Set the air fryer to 92°C for 1 minute, or until the butter is melted. Add the onions and salt to the pan.
Set the air fryer to 92°C for 15 minutes, or until onions are softened.
Set the air fryer to 192°C for 15 minutes, until onions are a deep golden brown, stirring two or three times during the cooking time. Let cool completely.
In a medium bowl, stir together the cooked onions, soft white cheese, sour cream, onion powder, and chives. Season with salt and pepper. Cover and refrigerate for 2 hours to allow the flavours to blend.
Serve the dip with potato crisps or vegetable crisps.

# Spiced Roasted Cashews

**Prep time: 5 minutes | Cook time: 10 minutes | Serves 4**

475 ml raw cashews
2 tablespoons olive oil
¼ teaspoon salt

¼ teaspoon chilli powder
⅛ teaspoon garlic powder
⅛ teaspoon smoked paprika

Preheat the air fryer to 182°C.
In a large bowl, toss all of the ingredients together.
Pour the cashews into the air fryer basket and roast them for 5 minutes. Shake the basket, then cook for 5 minutes more.
Serve immediately.

# Old Bay Chicken Wings

**Prep time: 10 minutes | Cook time: 12 to 15 minutes | Serves 4**

2 tablespoons Old Bay or all-purpose seasoning
2 teaspoons baking powder

2 teaspoons salt
900 g chicken wings, patted dry
Cooking spray

Preheat the air fryer to 204°C. Lightly spray the air fryer basket with cooking spray.
Combine the seasoning, baking powder, and salt in a large zip-top plastic bag. Add the chicken wings, seal, and shake until the wings are thoroughly coated in the seasoning mixture.
Lay the chicken wings in the air fryer basket in a single layer and lightly mist with cooking spray. You may need to work in batches to avoid overcrowding.
Air fry for 12 to 15 minutes, flipping the wings halfway through, or until the wings are lightly browned and the internal temperature reaches at least 74°C on a meat thermometer.
Remove from the basket to a plate and repeat with the remaining chicken wings.
Serve hot.

# Authentic Scotch Eggs

**Prep time: 15 minutes | Cook time: 11 to 13 minutes | Serves 6**

680 g bulk lean chicken or turkey sausage
3 raw eggs, divided
355 ml dried breadcrumbs,

divided
120 ml plain flour
6 hardboiled eggs, peeled
Cooking oil spray

In a large bowl, combine the chicken sausage, 1 raw egg, and 120 ml of breadcrumbs and mix well. Divide the mixture into 6 pieces and flatten each into a long oval.
In a shallow bowl, beat the remaining 2 raw eggs.
Place the flour in a small bowl.
Place the remaining 240 ml of breadcrumbs in a second small bowl.
Roll each hardboiled egg in the flour and wrap one of the chicken sausage pieces around each egg to encircle it completely.
One at a time, roll the encased eggs in the flour, dip in the beaten eggs, and finally dip in the breadcrumbs to coat.
Insert the crisper plate into the basket and the basket into the unit.
Preheat the unit by selecting AIR FRY, setting the temperature to 192°C, and setting the time to 3 minutes. Select START/STOP to begin.
Once the unit is preheated, spray the crisper plate with cooking oil. Place the eggs in a single layer into the basket and spray them with oil.
Select AIR FRY, set the temperature to 192°C, and set the time to 13 minutes. Select START/STOP to begin.1After about 6 minutes, use tongs to turn the eggs and spray them with more oil. Resume cooking for 5 to 7 minutes more, or until the chicken is thoroughly cooked and the Scotch eggs are browned.1When the cooking is complete, serve warm.

# Easy Roasted Chickpeas

**Prep time: 5 minutes | Cook time: 15 minutes | Makes about 240 ml**

1 (425 g) can chickpeas, drained
2 teaspoons curry powder

¼ teaspoon salt
1 tablespoon olive oil

Drain chickpeas thoroughly and spread in a single layer on paper towels. Cover with another paper towel and press gently to remove extra moisture. Don't press too hard or you'll crush the chickpeas.
Mix curry powder and salt together.
Place chickpeas in a medium bowl and sprinkle with seasonings. Stir well to coat.
Add olive oil and stir again to distribute oil.
Air fry at 200°C for 15 minutes, stopping to shake basket about halfway through cooking time.
Cool completely and store in airtight container.

# Parmesan French Fries

**Prep time: 10 minutes | Cook time: 15 minutes per batch | Serves 2**

2 to 3 large russet or Maris Piper potatoes, peeled and cut into ½-inch sticks
2 teaspoons vegetable or rapeseed oil
177 ml grated Parmesan cheese

½ teaspoon salt
Freshly ground black pepper, to taste
1 teaspoon fresh chopped parsley

Bring a large saucepan of salted water to a boil on the stovetop while you peel and cut the potatoes. Blanch the potatoes in the boiling salted water for 4 minutes while you preheat the air fryer to 204°C. Strain the potatoes and rinse them with cold water. Dry them well with a clean kitchen towel.
Toss the dried potato sticks gently with the oil and place them in the air fryer basket. Air fry for 25 minutes, shaking the basket a few times while the fries cook to help them brown evenly.
Combine the Parmesan cheese, salt and pepper. With 2 minutes left on the air fryer cooking time, sprinkle the fries with the Parmesan cheese mixture. Toss the fries to coat them evenly with the cheese mixture and continue to air fry for the final 2 minutes, until the cheese has melted and just starts to brown.
Sprinkle the finished fries with chopped parsley, a little more grated Parmesan cheese if you like, and serve.

## Stuffed Fried Mushrooms

**Prep time: 20 minutes | Cook time: 10 to 11 minutes | Serves 10**

120 ml panko breadcrumbs
½ teaspoon freshly ground black pepper
½ teaspoon onion powder
½ teaspoon cayenne pepper

1 (227 g) package soft white cheese, at room temperature
20 cremini or button mushrooms, stemmed
1 to 2 tablespoons oil

In a medium bowl, whisk the breadcrumbs, black pepper, onion powder, and cayenne until blended.
Add the soft white cheese and mix until well blended. Fill each mushroom top with 1 teaspoon of the soft white cheese mixture
Preheat the air fryer to 182°C. Line the air fryer basket with a piece of parchment paper.
Place the mushrooms on the parchment and spritz with oil.
Cook for 5 minutes. Shake the basket and cook for 5 to 6 minutes more until the filling is firm and the mushrooms are soft.

## Black Bean Corn Dip

**Prep time: 10 minutes | Cook time: 10 minutes | Serves 4**

½ (425 g) can black beans, drained and rinsed
½ (425 g) can corn, drained and rinsed
60 ml chunky salsa
57 g low-fat soft white cheese

60 ml shredded low-fat Cheddar cheese
½ teaspoon ground cumin
½ teaspoon paprika
Salt and freshly ground black pepper, to taste

Preheat the air fryer to 164°C.
In a medium bowl, mix together the black beans, corn, salsa, soft white cheese, Cheddar cheese, cumin, and paprika. Season with salt and pepper and stir until well combined.
Spoon the mixture into a baking dish.
Place baking dish in the air fryer basket and bake until heated through, about 10 minutes.
Serve hot.

## Crunchy Basil White Beans

**Prep time: 2 minutes | Cook time: 19 minutes | Serves 2**

1 (425 g) can cooked white beans
2 tablespoons olive oil
1 teaspoon fresh sage, chopped

¼ teaspoon garlic powder
¼ teaspoon salt, divided
1 teaspoon chopped fresh basil

Preheat the air fryer to 192°C.
In a medium bowl, mix together the beans, olive oil, sage, garlic, ⅛ teaspoon salt, and basil.
Pour the white beans into the air fryer and spread them out in a single layer.
Bake for 10 minutes. Stir and continue cooking for an additional 5 to 9 minutes, or until they reach your preferred level of crispiness.
Toss with the remaining ⅛ teaspoon salt before serving.

## Pepperoni Pizza Dip

**Prep time: 10 minutes | Cook time: 10 minutes | Serves 6**

170 g soft white cheese
177 ml shredded Italian cheese blend
60 ml sour cream
1½ teaspoons dried Italian seasoning
¼ teaspoon garlic salt
¼ teaspoon onion powder
177 ml pizza sauce

120 ml sliced miniature pepperoni
60 ml sliced black olives
1 tablespoon thinly sliced green onion
Cut-up raw vegetables, toasted baguette slices, pitta chips, or tortilla chips, for serving

In a small bowl, combine the soft white cheese, 60 ml of the shredded cheese, the sour cream, Italian seasoning, garlic salt, and onion powder. Stir until smooth and the ingredients are well blended.
Spread the mixture in a baking pan. Top with the pizza sauce, spreading to the edges. Sprinkle with the remaining 120 ml shredded cheese. Arrange the pepperoni slices on top of the cheese. Top with the black olives and green onion.
Place the pan in the air fryer basket. Set the air fryer to 176°C for 10 minutes, or until the pepperoni is beginning to brown on the edges and the cheese is bubbly and lightly browned.
Let stand for 5 minutes before serving with vegetables, toasted baguette slices, pitta chips, or tortilla chips.

## Lemon Shrimp with Garlic Olive Oil

**Prep time: 5 minutes | Cook time: 6 minutes | Serves 4**

454 g medium shrimp, cleaned and deveined
60 ml plus 2 tablespoons olive oil, divided
Juice of ½ lemon
3 garlic cloves, minced and divided

½ teaspoon salt
¼ teaspoon red pepper flakes
Lemon wedges, for serving (optional)
Marinara sauce, for dipping (optional)

Preheat the air fryer to 192°C.
In a large bowl, combine the shrimp with 2 tablespoons of the olive oil, as well as the lemon juice, ⅓ of the minced garlic, salt, and red pepper flakes. Toss to coat the shrimp well.
In a small ramekin, combine the remaining 60 ml of olive oil and the remaining minced garlic.
Tear off a 12-by-12-inch sheet of aluminium foil. Pour the shrimp into the centre of the foil, then fold the sides up and crimp the edges so that it forms an aluminium foil bowl that is open on top. Place this packet into the air fryer basket.
Roast the shrimp for 4 minutes, then open the air fryer and place the ramekin with oil and garlic in the basket beside the shrimp packet. Cook for 2 more minutes.
Transfer the shrimp on a serving plate or platter with the ramekin of garlic olive oil on the side for dipping. You may also serve with lemon wedges and marinara sauce, if desired.

# Shishito Peppers with Herb Dressing

**Prep time: 10 minutes | Cook time: 6 minutes | Serves 2 to 4**

170 g shishito or Padron peppers
1 tablespoon vegetable oil
Rock salt and freshly ground black pepper, to taste
120 ml mayonnaise
2 tablespoons finely chopped fresh basil leaves
2 tablespoons finely chopped

fresh flat-leaf parsley
1 tablespoon finely chopped fresh tarragon
1 tablespoon finely chopped fresh chives
Finely grated zest of ½ lemon
1 tablespoon fresh lemon juice
Flaky sea salt, for serving

Preheat the air fryer to 204ºC.
In a bowl, toss together the shishitos and oil to evenly coat and season with rock salt and black pepper. Transfer to the air fryer and air fry for 6 minutes, shaking the basket halfway through, or until the shishitos are blistered and lightly charred.
Meanwhile, in a small bowl, whisk together the mayonnaise, basil, parsley, tarragon, chives, lemon zest, and lemon juice.
Pile the peppers on a plate, sprinkle with flaky sea salt, and serve hot with the dressing.

# Grilled Ham and Cheese on Raisin Bread

**Prep time: 5 minutes | Cook time: 10 minutes | Serves 1**

2 slices raisin bread or fruit loaf
2 tablespoons butter, softened
2 teaspoons honey mustard
3 slices thinly sliced honey roast

ham (about 85 g)
4 slices Muenster cheese (about 85 g)
2 toothpicks

Preheat the air fryer to 188ºC.
Spread the softened butter on one side of both slices of bread and place the bread, buttered side down on the counter. Spread the honey mustard on the other side of each slice of bread.
Layer 2 slices of cheese, the ham and the remaining 2 slices of cheese on one slice of bread and top with the other slice of bread. Remember to leave the buttered side of the bread on the outside.
Transfer the sandwich to the air fryer basket and secure the sandwich with toothpicks.
Air fry for 5 minutes. Flip the sandwich over, remove the toothpicks and air fry for another 5 minutes. Cut the sandwich in half and enjoy!

# Greens Chips with Curried Yoghurt Sauce

**Prep time: 10 minutes | Cook time: 5 to 6 minutes | Serves 4**

240 ml low-fat Greek yoghurt
1 tablespoon freshly squeezed lemon juice
1 tablespoon curry powder
½ bunch curly kale, stemmed, ribs removed and discarded,

leaves cut into 2- to 3-inch pieces
½ bunch chard, stemmed, ribs removed and discarded, leaves cut into 2- to 3-inch pieces
1½ teaspoons olive oil

In a small bowl, stir together the yoghurt, lemon juice, and curry powder. Set aside.
In a large bowl, toss the kale and chard with the olive oil, working the oil into the leaves with your hands. This helps break up the fibres in the leaves so the chips are tender.
Air fry the greens in batches at 200ºC for 5 to 6 minutes, until crisp, shaking the basket once during cooking. Serve with the yoghurt sauce.

# Tangy Fried Pickle Spears

**Prep time: 5 minutes | Cook time: 15 minutes | Serves 6**

2 jars sweet and sour pickle spears, patted dry
2 medium-sized eggs
80 ml milk
1 teaspoon garlic powder

1 teaspoon sea salt
½ teaspoon shallot powder
⅓ teaspoon chilli powder
80 ml plain flour
Cooking spray

Preheat the air fryer to 196ºC. Spritz the air fryer basket with cooking spray.
In a bowl, beat together the eggs with milk. In another bowl, combine garlic powder, sea salt, shallot powder, chilli powder and plain flour until well blended.
One by one, roll the pickle spears in the powder mixture, then dredge them in the egg mixture. Dip them in the powder mixture a second time for additional coating.
Arrange the coated pickles in the prepared basket. Air fry for 15 minutes until golden and crispy, shaking the basket halfway through to ensure even cooking.
Transfer to a plate and let cool for 5 minutes before serving.

# Egg Roll Pizza Sticks

**Prep time: 10 minutes | Cook time: 5 minutes | Serves 4**

Olive oil
8 pieces low-fat string cheese
8 egg roll wrappers or spring roll pastry

24 slices turkey pepperoni or salami
Marinara sauce, for dipping (optional)

Spray the air fryer basket lightly with olive oil. Fill a small bowl with water.
Place each egg roll wrapper diagonally on a work surface. It should look like a diamond.
Place 3 slices of turkey pepperoni in a vertical line down the centre of the wrapper.
Place 1 Mozzarella cheese stick on top of the turkey pepperoni.
Fold the top and bottom corners of the egg roll wrapper over the cheese stick.
Fold the left corner over the cheese stick and roll the cheese stick up to resemble a spring roll. Dip a finger in the water and seal the edge of the roll
Repeat with the rest of the pizza sticks.
Place them in the air fryer basket in a single layer, making sure to leave a little space between each one. Lightly spray the pizza sticks with oil. You may need to cook these in batches.
Air fry at 192ºC until the pizza sticks are lightly browned and crispy, about 5 minutes.1These are best served hot while the cheese is melted. Accompany with a small bowl of marinara sauce, if desired.

# String Bean Fries

**Prep time: 15 minutes | Cook time: 5 to 6 minutes | Serves 4**

227 g fresh green beans
2 eggs
4 teaspoons water
120 ml white flour
120 ml breadcrumbs

¼ teaspoon salt
¼ teaspoon ground black pepper
¼ teaspoon mustard powder (optional)
Oil for misting or cooking spray

Preheat the air fryer to 182°C.
Trim stem ends from green beans, wash, and pat dry.
In a shallow dish, beat eggs and water together until well blended.
Place flour in a second shallow dish.
In a third shallow dish, stir together the breadcrumbs, salt, pepper, and dry mustard if using.
Dip each bean in egg mixture, flour, egg mixture again, then breadcrumbs.
When you finish coating all the green beans, open air fryer and place them in basket.
Cook for 3 minutes.
Stop and mist green beans with oil or cooking spray.1Cook for 2 to 3 more minutes or until green beans are crispy and nicely browned.

# Chapter 9 Staples, Sauces, Dips, and Dressings

# Chapter 9 Staples, Sauces, Dips, and Dressings

## Blue Cheese Dressing

**Prep time: 5 minutes | Cook time: 0 minutes | Serves 12**

180 ml sugar-free mayonnaise
60 ml sour cream
120 ml double cream
1 teaspoon minced garlic
1 tablespoon freshly squeezed
lemon juice

1 tablespoon apple cider vinegar
1 teaspoon hot sauce
½ teaspoon sea salt
110 g blue cheese, crumbled
(about 180 ml)

In a medium bowl, whisk together the mayonnaise, sour cream, and double cream.
Stir in the garlic, lemon juice, apple cider vinegar, hot sauce, and sea salt.
Add the blue cheese crumbles and stir until well combined.
Transfer to an airtight container and refrigerate for up to 1 week.

## Italian Dressing

**Prep time: 5 minutes | Cook time: 0 minutes | Serves 12**

60 ml red wine vinegar
120 ml extra-virgin olive oil
¼ teaspoon salt
¼ teaspoon freshly ground black
pepper

1 teaspoon dried Italian
seasoning
1 teaspoon Dijon mustard
1 garlic clove, minced

In a small jar, combine the vinegar, olive oil, salt, pepper, Italian seasoning, mustard, and garlic.
Close with a tight-fitting lid and shake vigorously for 1 minute.
Refrigerate for up to 1 week.

## Air Fryer Artichoke Dip

**Prep time: 15 minutes | Cook time: 0 minutes | Serves 3**

1 (400 g) can artichoke hearts,
drained
450 g goat cheese
2 tablespoons extra-virgin olive
oil
2 teaspoons lemon juice
1 garlic clove, minced
1 tablespoon chopped parsley
1 tablespoon chopped chives

½ tablespoon chopped basil
½ teaspoon sea salt
½ teaspoon freshly ground black
pepper
Dash of cayenne pepper
(optional)
120 ml freshly grated Pecorino
Romano

In a food processor, combine all the ingredients, except the Pecorino Romano, and process until well incorporated and creamy.

Top with the freshly grated Pecorino Romano.
Store in an airtight container in the refrigerator for up to 3 days.

## Gochujang Dip

**Prep time: 5 minutes | Cook time: 0 minutes | Serves 4**

2 tablespoons gochujang
(Korean red pepper paste)
1 tablespoon mayonnaise
1 tablespoon toasted sesame oil

1 tablespoon minced fresh
ginger
1 tablespoon minced garlic
1 teaspoon agave nectar

In a small bowl, combine the gochujang, mayonnaise, sesame oil, ginger, garlic, and agave. Stir until well combined.
Use immediately or store in the refrigerator, covered, for up to 3 days.

## Sweet Ginger Teriyaki Sauce

**Prep time: 5 minutes | Cook time: 0 minutes | Serves 4**

60 ml pineapple juice
60 ml low-salt soy sauce
2 tablespoons packed brown
sugar

1 tablespoon arrowroot powder
or corn flour
1 tablespoon grated fresh ginger
1 teaspoon garlic powder

Mix together all the ingredients in a small bowl and whisk to incorporate.
Serve immediately, or transfer to an airtight container and refrigerate until ready to use.

## Cucumber Yoghurt Dip

**Prep time: 5 minutes | Cook time: 0 minutes | Serves 2 to 3**

235 ml plain, unsweetened, full-
fat Greek yoghurt
120 ml cucumber, peeled,
seeded, and diced
1 tablespoon freshly squeezed

lemon juice
1 tablespoon chopped fresh mint
1 small garlic clove, minced
Salt and freshly ground black
pepper, to taste

In a food processor, combine the yoghurt, cucumber, lemon juice, mint, and garlic.
Pulse several times to combine, leaving noticeable cucumber chunks.
Taste and season with salt and pepper.

# Pecan Tartar Sauce

**Prep time: 10 minutes | Cook time: 10 minutes | Makes 300 ml**

4 tablespoons pecans, finely chopped
120 ml sour cream
120 ml mayonnaise
½ teaspoon grated lemon zest
1½ tablespoons freshly

squeezed lemon juice
2½ tablespoons chopped fresh parsley
1 teaspoon paprika
2 tablespoons chopped dill pickle

Preheat the air fryer to 164°C.
Spread the pecans in a single layer on a parchment sheet lightly spritzed with oil.
Place the pecans in the air fryer. Air fry for 7 to 10 minutes, stirring every 2 minutes. Let cool.
In a medium bowl, mix the sour cream, mayonnaise, lemon zest, and lemon juice until blended. Stir in the parsley paprika, dill pickle, and pecans.
Cover and refrigerate to chill for at least 1 hour to blend the flavours. This sauce should be used within 2 weeks.

# Red Buffalo Sauce

**Prep time: 5 minutes | Cook time: 20 minutes | Makes 475 ml**

60 ml olive oil
4 garlic cloves, roughly chopped
1 (142 g) small red onion, roughly chopped
6 red chillies, roughly chopped (about 56 g in total)

235 ml water
120 ml apple cider vinegar
½ teaspoon salt
½ teaspoon freshly ground black pepper

In a large non-stick sauté pan, heat 60 ml olive oil over medium-high heat. Once it's hot, add the garlic, onion, and chillies.
Cook for 5 minutes, stirring occasionally, until onions are golden brown. Add the water and bring to a boil. Cook for about 10 minutes or until the water has nearly evaporated.
Transfer the cooked onion and chili mixture to a food processor or blender and blend briefly to combine. Add the apple cider vinegar, salt, and pepper. Blend again for 30 seconds.
Using a mesh sieve, strain the sauce into a bowl. Use a spoon or spatula to scrape and press all the liquid from the pulp.

# Peachy Barbecue Sauce

**Prep time: 10 minutes | Cook time: 0 minutes | Makes 535 ml**

235 ml peach preserve
235 ml ketchup
2 tablespoons apple cider vinegar
2 tablespoons light brown sugar

1 teaspoon chilli powder
½ teaspoon freshly ground black pepper
½ teaspoon dry mustard

In a medium bowl, stir together the peach preserve, ketchup, and vinegar until blended. In a small bowl, whisk the brown sugar, chilli powder, pepper, and dry mustard to combine.
Add the brown sugar mixture to the peach preserves mixture. Mix well to combine.
Transfer the barbecue sauce to an airtight container.
Refrigerate for up to 1 week until ready to use as a sauce or marinade.

# Cauliflower Alfredo Sauce

**Prep time: 2 minutes | Cook time: 0 minutes | Makes 1 L**

2 tablespoons olive oil
6 garlic cloves, minced
700 ml unsweetened almond milk
1 (450 g) head cauliflower, cut into florets

1 teaspoon salt
¼ teaspoon freshly ground black pepper
Juice of 1 lemon
4 tablespoons Engevita yeast flakes

In a medium saucepan, heat the olive oil over medium-high heat.
Add the garlic and sauté for 1 minute or until fragrant. Add the almond milk, stir, and bring to a boil. Gently add the cauliflower. Stir in the salt and pepper and return to a boil.
Continue cooking over medium-high heat for 5 minutes or until the cauliflower is soft. Stir frequently and reduce heat if needed to prevent the liquid from boiling over.
Carefully transfer the cauliflower and cooking liquid to a food processor, using a slotted spoon to scoop out the larger pieces of cauliflower before pouring in the liquid.
Add the lemon and yeast flakes and blend for 1 to 2 minutes until smooth. Serve immediately.

# Chapter 10 Holiday Specials

# Chapter 10 Holiday Specials

## Kale Salad Sushi Rolls with Sriracha Mayonnaise

**Prep time: 10 minutes | Cook time: 10 minutes | Serves 12**

Kale Salad:
350 ml chopped kale
1 tablespoon sesame seeds
¾ teaspoon soy sauce
¾ teaspoon toasted sesame oil
½ teaspoon rice vinegar
¼ teaspoon ginger
⅛ teaspoon garlic powder
Sushi Rolls:

3 sheets sushi nori
1 batch cauliflower rice
½ avocado, sliced
Sriracha Mayonnaise:
60 ml Sriracha sauce
60 ml vegan mayonnaise
Coating:
120 ml panko breadcrumbs

Preheat the air fryer to 200°C.
In a medium bowl, toss all the ingredients for the salad together until well coated and set aside.
Place a sheet of nori on a clean work surface and spread the cauliflower rice in an even layer on the nori. Scoop 2 to 3 tablespoon of kale salad on the rice and spread over. Place 1 or 2 avocado slices on top. Roll up the sushi, pressing gently to get a nice, tight roll. Repeat to make the remaining 2 rolls.
In a bowl, stir together the Sriracha sauce and mayonnaise until smooth. Add breadcrumbs to a separate bowl. Dredge the sushi rolls in Sriracha Mayonnaise, then roll in breadcrumbs till well coated.
Place the coated sushi rolls in the air fryer basket and air fry for 10 minutes, or until golden brown and crispy. Flip the sushi rolls gently halfway through to ensure even cooking.
Transfer to a platter and rest for 5 minutes before slicing each roll into 8 pieces. Serve warm.

## Lemony and Garlicky Asparagus

**Prep time: 5 minutes | Cook time: 10 minutes | Makes 10 spears**

10 spears asparagus (about 230 g in total), snap the ends off
1 tablespoon lemon juice
2 teaspoons minced garlic

½ teaspoon salt
¼ teaspoon ground black pepper
Cooking spray

Preheat the air fryer to 204°C.
Line a parchment paper in the air fryer basket.
Put the asparagus spears in a large bowl. Drizzle with lemon juice and sprinkle with minced garlic, salt, and ground black pepper. Toss to coat well.
Transfer the asparagus in the preheated air fryer and spritz with cooking spray.
Air fryer for 10 minutes or until wilted and soft. Flip the asparagus halfway through.
Serve immediately.

## Southwest Corn and Pepper Roast

**Prep time: 10 minutes | Cook time: 10 minutes | Serves 4**

For the Corn:
350 ml thawed frozen corn kernels
235 ml mixed diced peppers
1 jalapeño, diced
235 ml diced brown onion
½ teaspoon ancho chilli powder
1 tablespoon fresh lemon juice

1 teaspoon ground cumin
½ teaspoon rock salt
Cooking spray
For Serving:
60 ml feta cheese
60 ml chopped fresh coriander
1 tablespoon fresh lemon juice

Preheat the air fryer to 192°C.
Spritz the air fryer with cooking spray. Combine the ingredients for the corn in a large bowl. Stir to mix well.
Pour the mixture into the air fryer. Air fry for 10 minutes or until the corn and peppers are soft. Shake the basket halfway through the cooking time.
Transfer them onto a large plate, then spread with feta cheese and coriander. Drizzle with lemon juice and serve.

## Golden Nuggets

**Prep time: 15 minutes | Cook time: 4 minutes per batch | Makes 20 nuggets**

235 ml plain flour, plus more for dusting
1 teaspoon baking powder
½ teaspoon butter, at room temperature, plus more for brushing

¼ teaspoon salt
60 ml water
⅛ teaspoon onion powder
¼ teaspoon garlic powder
⅛ teaspoon seasoning salt
Cooking spray

Preheat the air fryer to 188°C. Line the air fryer basket with parchment paper.
Mix the flour, baking powder, butter, and salt in a large bowl. Stir to mix well. Gradually whisk in the water until a sanity dough forms.
Put the dough on a lightly floured work surface, then roll it out into a ½-inch thick rectangle with a rolling pin.
Cut the dough into about twenty 1- or 2-inch squares, then arrange the squares in a single layer in the preheated air fryer. Spritz with cooking spray.
You need to work in batches to avoid overcrowding. Combine onion powder, garlic powder, and seasoning salt in a small bowl. Stir to mix well, then sprinkle the squares with the powder mixture.
Air fry the dough squares for 4 minutes or until golden brown. Flip the squares halfway through the cooking time.
Remove the golden nuggets from the air fryer and brush with more butter immediately. Serve warm.

## Garlicky Zoodles

**Prep time: 10 minutes | Cook time: 10 minutes | Serves 4**

2 large courgette, peeled and spiralized
2 large yellow butternut squash, peeled and spiralized
1 tablespoon olive oil, divided

½ teaspoon rock salt
1 garlic clove, whole
2 tablespoons fresh basil, chopped
Cooking spray

Preheat the air fryer to 182°C. Spritz the air fryer basket with cooking spray.

Combine the courgette and butternut squash with 1 teaspoon olive oil and salt in a large bowl. Toss to coat well.

Transfer the courgette and butternut squash in the preheated air fryer and add the garlic. Air fry for 10 minutes or until tender and fragrant. Toss the spiralized courgette and butternut squash halfway through the cooking time.

Transfer the cooked courgette and butternut squash onto a plate and set aside. Remove the garlic from the air fryer and allow to cool for a few minutes.

Mince the garlic and combine with remaining olive oil in a small bowl. Stir to mix well.

Drizzle the spiralized courgette and butternut squash with garlic oil and sprinkle with basil. Toss to serve.

## Eggnog Bread

**Prep time: 10 minutes | Cook time: 18 minutes | Serves 6 to 8**

235 ml flour, plus more for dusting
60 ml sugar
1 teaspoon baking powder
¼ teaspoon salt
¼ teaspoon nutmeg
120 ml eggnog
1 egg yolk

1 tablespoon plus 1 teaspoon butter, melted
60 ml pecans
60 ml chopped candied fruit (cherries, pineapple, or mixed fruits)
Cooking spray

Preheat the air fryer to 182°C.

In a medium bowl, stir together the flour, sugar, baking powder, salt, and nutmeg. Add eggnog, egg yolk, and butter. Mix well but do not beat. Stir in nuts and fruit.

Spray a baking pan with cooking spray and dust with flour. Spread batter into prepared pan and bake for 18 minutes or until top is dark golden brown and bread starts to pull away from sides of pan.

Serve immediately.

## Garlicky Knots with Parsley

**Prep time: 10 minutes | Cook time: 10 minutes | Makes 8 knots**

1 teaspoon dried parsley
60 ml melted butter
2 teaspoons garlic powder

1 (312 g) tube refrigerated French bread dough, cut into 8 slices

Preheat the air fryer to 176°C.

Combine the parsley, butter, and garlic powder in a bowl. Stir to

mix well. Place the French bread dough slices on a clean work surface, then roll each slice into a 6-inch-long rope.

Tie the ropes into knots and arrange them on a plate. Brush the knots with butter mixture. Transfer the knots into the air fryer.

You need to work in batches to avoid overcrowding. Air fry for 5 minutes or until the knots are golden brown. Flip the knots halfway through the cooking time. Serve immediately.

## Air Fried Spicy Olives

**Prep time: 10 minutes | Cook time: 5 minutes | Serves 4**

340 g pitted black extra-large olives
60 ml plain flour
235 ml panko breadcrumbs
2 teaspoons dried thyme

1 teaspoon red pepper flakes
1 teaspoon smoked paprika
1 egg beaten with 1 tablespoon water
Vegetable oil for spraying

Preheat the air fryer to 204°C.

Drain the olives and place them on a paper towel–lined plate to dry. Put the flour on a plate.

Combine the panko, thyme, red pepper flakes, and paprika on a separate plate. Dip an olive in the flour, shaking off any excess, then coat with egg mixture.

Dredge the olive in the panko mixture, pressing to make the crumbs adhere, and place the breaded olive on a platter. Repeat with the remaining olives.

Spray the olives with oil and place them in a single layer in the air fryer basket. Work in batches if necessary so as not to overcrowd the basket. Air fry for 5 minutes until the breading is browned and crispy.

Serve warm

## Teriyaki Shrimp Skewers

**Prep time: 10 minutes | Cook time: 6 minutes | Makes 12 skewered shrimp**

1½ tablespoons mirin
1½ teaspoons ginger paste
1½ tablespoons soy sauce
12 large shrimp, peeled and

deveined
1 large egg
180 ml panko breadcrumbs
Cooking spray

Combine the mirin, ginger paste, and soy sauce in a large bowl. Stir to mix well.

Dunk the shrimp in the bowl of mirin mixture, then wrap the bowl in plastic and refrigerate for 1 hour to marinate.

Preheat the air fryer to 204°C. Spritz the air fryer basket with cooking spray.

Run twelve 4-inch skewers through each shrimp.

Whisk the egg in the bowl of marinade to combine well. Pour the breadcrumbs on a plate. Dredge the shrimp skewers in the egg mixture, then shake the excess off and roll over the breadcrumbs to coat well.

Arrange the shrimp skewers in the preheated air fryer and spritz with cooking spray. You need to work in batches to avoid overcrowding.

Air fry for 6 minutes or until the shrimp are opaque and firm. Flip the shrimp skewers halfway through.

Serve immediately.

# Crispy Green Tomato Slices

**Prep time: 10 minutes | Cook time: 8 minutes | Makes 12 slices**

120 ml plain flour
1 egg
120 ml buttermilk
235 ml cornmeal
235 ml panko breadcrumbs

2 green tomatoes, cut into ¼-inch-thick slices, patted dry
½ teaspoon salt
½ teaspoon ground black pepper
Cooking spray

Preheat the air fryer to 204°C.

Line the air fryer basket with parchment paper.

Pour the flour in a bowl. Whisk the egg and buttermilk in a second bowl. Combine the cornmeal and panko breadcrumbs in a third bowl.

Dredge the tomato slices in the bowl of flour first, then into the egg mixture, and then dunk the slices into the cornmeal mixture. Shake the excess off.

Transfer the well-coated tomato slices in the preheated air fryer and sprinkle with salt and ground black pepper. Spritz the tomato slices with cooking spray.

Air fry for 8 minutes or until crispy and lightly browned. Flip the slices halfway through the cooking time.

Serve immediately.

Printed in Great Britain
by Amazon

11629282R00045